W9-CIK-143

The AGE of ERROR

By

W. E. MICHAEL, A.B., L.L.B.

Foreword by Senator Richard B. Russell

GREENWOOD PRESS, PUBLISHERS
WESTPORT, CONNECTICUT

Library of Congress Cataloging in Publication Data

Michael, W   E   1904-
    The age of error.

    Reprint of the 1957 ed. published by Vantage Press,
New York.
    1. Segregation in education--Southern States.
2. Negroes--Education--Southern States. I. Title.
[LC212.522.S7M5 1977]   370.19'344   77-4233
ISBN 0-8371-9588-8

Originally published in 1957 by Vantage Press, Inc., New York

Reprinted with the permission of W. E. Michael

Reprinted in 1977 by Greenwood Press, Inc.

Library of Congress catalog card number 77-4233

ISBN 0-8371-9588-8

Printed in the United States of America

FOREWORD

The momentous decision by the United States Supreme Court in the school cases handed down on May 17, 1954, has brought many problems to our country. For the first time in its history, our highest Court abandoned law and precedent as a basis of legal ruling, and undertook to wipe out the Constitutions and laws of many States by a decision based on the writings and reasoning of psychologists and pseudopsychologists. This decision was followed by others which have caused constitutional authorities in every section of our country grave concern for the future of the American system which has heretofore been based on the division of powers between the three branches of the federal government, as well as for our dual system of government which had formerly recognized that the powers of the federal government were limited and that the several States could exercise the rights and powers guaranteed to them by the Tenth provision of our Bill of Rights.

No one can with certainty predict the final consequences of the Court's abandonment of precedent, nullification of the doctrine of *stare decisis,* and seizure of legislative power.

We know, however, from the atmosphere generated by this decision that it has all but destroyed the cordial racial relations in those States where the races are more equal in number, relations that have been painfully and painstakingly built by men of good will of both races in the more than nine decades since Appomattox. It is also clear that many of the States do not intend to surrender their constitutional rights as legal entities if ways can be found to maintain State authority in those fields where the States have always claimed predominance.

iii

The deep feeling on both sides of the question has been expressed by many authors. In my opinion, *The Age of Error* by Mr. W. E. Michael of Sweetwater, Tennessee, is one of the most helpful to an understanding of the grave issues presented. In *The Age of Error* Mr. Michael deals with this subject not only from the standpoint of the legal question involved but, more important, discusses with great clarity the human reactions of those most vitally affected.

The author has traveled widely, and his experience helps him to present the naïveté of many of those living in sections of the country where there is no real racial problem. I understand that the community in which Mr. Michael lives will not be as greatly affected by the decision as most areas in the deep South, but he has evidenced a deep understanding of this grave problem and the evil consequences which will inevitably flow from the decision.

Mr. Michael deals factually and calmly with issues which have been the subject of a great deal of intemperance by many writers on either side. I think that his book will be a material contribution to a better understanding of the real issues involved.

October 25, 1956

RICHARD B. RUSSELL

THE SUPREME COURT
JUMPS THE CONSTITUTIONAL FENCE

INTRODUCTION

Fable has it that the mice, greatly agitated by the inroads a certain cat was making upon the mouse population, met in solemn conclave and after much thought concluded that the cat should be made to wear a bell to warn the mice of approaching danger. This solution was enthusiastically acclaimed. Upon further deliberation the grandiose plan was abandoned when no mouse could be found who would attempt to bell the cat, apparently concluding that it was a job for men, not for mice.

Who will stop the Supreme Court of the United States? It is running rampant, leaving in its devastated wake the broken fragments of the Ninth and Tenth Amendments to the Constitution of the United States, the constitutions and statutes of sixteen sovereign States of the Union, many former decisions of the United States Supreme Court, and the decisions of a half-hundred States and territorial courts.

In the last two years, the Supreme Court of the United States has solemnly adjudged:

1. That separate public schools could not be maintained by the States even though such States provided "separate but equal" facilities for the white and colored races. The Court so held in spite of the fact that the laws and the constitutions of many such States positively prohibit the intermingling of the races in the public schools supported by such States. The Supreme Court cited no valid constitutional authority for this far-reaching decision.

2. That the federal government alone had the right to legislate upon the subject of sedition and that State laws upon that subject were invalid. A majority of the States have passed laws dealing with treason or sedition involving either the States or federal governments, and some of these laws are as old as the Union itself. The Supreme Court cited no valid constitutional authority for this far-reaching decision.

3. That the City of New York could not discharge an employee in its school system for taking advantage of the so-called "immunity" of the Fifth Amendment on the question of his membership in the Communist party. The charter of the City of New York gave the city such authority. The laws of the State of New York recognized and did not prohibit the exercise of such authority by the city. The Supreme Court cited no valid constitutional authority for its invasion of the rights of the City of New York in the conduct of its schools.

4. That the States (in this case, North Carolina) could not require Negroes and whites to ride in separate compartments in sections of public vehicles, even in *intrastate* commerce, even though such an arrangement was required under the laws of the State of North Carolina. In this case, the Supreme Court abandoned its reliance upon *interstate* commerce as a ground for federal intervention and again cited no valid constitutional authority for intervening in the enforcement of local laws or customs.

5. That a State, again North Carolina, was required by decree of that Court to admit a Negro to its universities in violation of the laws of the State of North Carolina. The Supreme Court appears to rely upon the doctrine of "separate but equal" facilities when that doctrine will serve a certain purpose and then to abandon and "reject" such doctrine when it cannot be used as a prop to justify federal intervention in local matters.

6. That the Constitution denied to any person or race the right: to attend segregated schools; to live in segregated

publicly owned housing projects; to use a segregated golf course, park, or recreational facility if owned by a city, county, or other public body (federal ownership was not involved); or to attend a city owned theatre, even when operated by a private corporation.

The six instances just mentioned all deal with matters of local government and have always been considered as forbidden to the federal government under the provisions of the Tenth Amendment to the Constitution. The opinions of the Court are silent as to the method by which it surmounted the protecting fence of the Tenth Amendment to gambol in forbidden pastures.

Sandwiched among these decisions were many others of similar purport. All these decisions strike at the powers of State governments expressed in their respective constitutions and laws and safeguarded to the States by the fundamental law of the land. Why do we stand idle while our basic freedoms are being demolished? Could it be because some mysterious voice, of seeming authority, has said, "The Supreme Court has spoken," as if that magic phrase righted all wrongs and stilled all discussion? Whose voice is it? Before surrendering our historic rights, our present accomplishments, and our future hopes, let us honestly explore the whole question and boldly announce the result of such study. This, too, is a job for men.

This task requires that we study the reasons given by the Court in support of its desertion of time-honored precedent. We must inquire why it chose to follow the teachings of psychology textbooks written by reputed left-wing sympathizers rather than the authority of laws and interpretations proven by almost a century of sound judicial reasoning.

We should start our inquiry with certain undeniable truths constantly in mind:

1. *It is not wrong, or unpatriotic to analyze or question a decision of the United States Supreme Court upon a constitutional issue.*

2. The fact that "the Supreme Court has spoken" does

not make right out of wrong. It does not and, fortunately, cannot change the Constitution.

3.   The Supreme Court cannot have or acquire any authority except as granted by constitutional means. It cannot, as seems to be popularly accepted, "order" everyone to comply with the Court's philosophy. It can only "order" the parties or litigants in any case to comply with the decision of the Court in that particular case.

4.   Decisions of the Supreme Court are generally accepted as law by other courts. But these decisions are always subject to reversal or rejection by the Supreme Court.

5.   The Supreme Court of the United States cannot amend, modify, repeal, or ignore any provision of the Constitution of the United States.

6.   The Constitution cannot be changed by any court. The Constitution can be amended only by the process set forth in the Constitution.

7.   The Supreme Court can enact no law. The legislative branch of the government is the only body in the United States endowed with the authority to pass laws. The chief executive can suggest laws, can veto laws, or approve laws. The Congress can, by two-thirds majority, pass a law over the President's veto. A court has absolutely no authority to create a new law, regardless of how much it may wish to do so.

8.   Supreme Court judges are appointed for life. The personnel of the Court changes only by death, resignation, or retirement. Such changes occur slowly. Members of that Court are not subject to election or defeat by the people. The only checks upon the Court are through legislation by Congress and through the power of the President, with the advice and consent of the Senate, to appoint new justices to the Court.

The trend of the Supreme Court's opinion away from the constitutional authority of State and local government and toward an all-powerful central government poses a mortal threat to the historic freedoms which all America holds dear. We cannot long remain free if our legal rights and duties are to be interpreted according to the whim and caprice of men, be they psychologists or judges, rather than established and duly enacted laws.

This drastic and dangerous trend is perhaps best identified in the public mind with the decision in the school-integration cases. The decision of the Court in these cases was not limited to holding that it is lawful for children of white and Negro races to attend the same school. It did not, as many seem to believe, merely hold that integration of the races in public schools was legal. The Court held in effect that mixture of the races in public schools was a requirement of the Constitution and therefore a requirement of federal law. This opinion declared that the Supreme Court, in any case brought before it, would order enforced integration or mixture of the races in the public schools of the South, without regard to the constitutions or laws of those States.

This decision is much larger in scope than is generally believed. In theory the Court decided that no State could enact or enforce a law which required children of the white race and children of the Negro race to attend segregated schools. All such laws were declared invalid on the ground that they violated the provision of the Fourteenth Amendment that: "No State shall . . . deny to any person within its jurisdiction the equal protection of the law." The Court went much further: it held that separate schools having equal facilities denied "minority groups" equal protection of the law because such segregated schools (with equal facilities) were "inherently unequal." This finding was not based upon evidence but upon the authority of textbook writers.

The Court did not rest content with striking down the State and local laws; it indicated an intention to serve notice upon all and sundry that its new philosophy must be put into effect without appreciable delay. *This was a bold and unwarranted assumption of power.* According to this

decision any person may file a suit and compel his admission
to any school or public gathering place. Apparently the
Court meant to say only that the whites could not have
segregation; but it would seem to follow that the Negroes
also would not be allowed to have schools, parks, or recreational facilities of their own.

In order fully to appreciate the infirmities of this decision
it is necessary to understand the history and background of
the area to which the decision is directed. This requires a
working knowledge of the people affected and of their respective ways of life. It is not an academic inquiry into some
idealistic vacuum, but an effort to understand the mental
and physical make-up of southerners, white and Negro. To
understand their problems it is necessary to understand their
past experiences and their future hopes and fears. The way
of life of a people, upon which their institutions are founded,
is evolved from their history, traditions, laws, and customs.

These things are not easily disregarded. The legal and
moral aspects of enforced integration in the South must be
considered in the light of this historical setting. We are not
concerned with an academic discussion of so-called "liberalism" or "human rights." The basic human rights of both
whites and Negroes in the South are involved in a very
practical way, as we shall discuss in the application of federal force to the integration of the races in southern schools.

It is impossible to encompass the whole problem by one
effort. It is not only a moral and legal problem but an economic and practical one. To be sure that our feet are firmly
planted on solid ground, it is of first importance to insure
that our thoughts and actions are in keeping with the laws
that bind us together as a nation and as a people. This does
not imply that every decision of the Supreme Court of the
United States is "the law." The question is whether such
decision or series of decisions of any court are in keeping
with the constitutions and laws as adopted and enacted by
the people and their duly elected representatives. These
constitutions and statutes, and the interpretation of them by

the courts as accepted by the people and legislative bodies over a great period of time, constitutes the established law of the land. This is known as the "body of the law." Adherence to these principles is what is known in legal terms as *stare decisis.*

PART I

STARE DECISIS

One of the most serious indictments against the Court's decision in the school cases, as well as other recent cases, is that apparently the Court has completely abandoned the rule of *stare decisis*. *Stare decisis* is defined by the legal dictionary as follows: "The doctrine or principal that the decisions of the court should stand as precedents for future guidance. While even a single adjudication of the court, upon a question properly before it, is not to be questioned or disregarded except for the most cogent reasons, and then only in a case where it is plain that the judgment was the result of a mistaken view of the condition of the law applicable to the question, the doctrine of *stare decisis* is not without exceptions. It does not apply where it can be shown that the law has been misunderstood or misapplied, or where the former determination is evidently contrary to reason." Literally, the doctrine means, "It stands decided."

This rule to stand by former decisions and not to disturb settled points of law has long been observed by the courts of this land as a great equalizing and stabilizing force. On the strength of it, laws are enacted, court decisions are rendered, contracts are executed, indebtedness is created, and rights and remedies are declared. It is the beacon light of experience. Without it there would surely be uncertainty and probably chaos in the business of government, in the complexities of modern industry and commerce, and in the application and enforcement of law.

The courts have regarded it not only as a convenience but as a necessity.

This doctrine does not contemplate that every court decision should constitute an immovable landmark. By its very nature it contemplates that a bad decision could and should be reversed and supplanted by a good one. Its true meaning is that precedent, when once established by clear judicial reasoning consistent with the basic laws of the land and buttressed by the acquiescence of other court decisions, will not be disturbed, except upon the most compelling authority and for the most cogent reasons.

Lay citiens may not, at first glance, appreciate the great danger involved in the abandonment of this long established principle. But lawyers and courts will readily appreciate that jurisprudence without *stare decisis* is indeed a ship at sea without a rudder.

THE FOOLISH FIRE

The South is on fire. It is not a slow burn but a consuming flame that sears and scorches the souls of men. The tragedy of it is that it is an unnecessary conflagration, built upon the funeral pyre of other disasters and agitated by the winds of unceasing propaganda. It is being constantly refueled with a new supply of incendiary material piled higher and higher by the imps whose sole mission in life seems to be to stoke this fire.

Although for the moment the fire is contained within the boundaries of a dozen southern States comprising one-quarter of the nation, there is ever increasing evidence that the flames may soon spread, like a thousand separate grass fires, through the body politic, North, South, East, and West. From every section of the country and from every segment of society come the rumblings of discontent arising from the Supreme Court's current trend. It was the Supreme Court's decision in the school-integration cases that kindled the flame in the South. This is no indication that the southern people are any different from people in the other sections of the country. Instead, it means that they alone must live with the problems created by forced school integration. It is indeed tragic that the Court adopted a philosophy so far at variance with the fundamental law of our land and with the constitutions and ways of life of a great section of our people.

An equally great and equally tragic aspect of this unnecessary fire is that the very person for whose benefit it was allegedly kindled, the southern Negro, is the person who will be burned the worst by it and who stands to lose the most from the activities of his alleged "benefactors," who

17

have but slight and passing interest in him but would like to exploit him for their own pernicious political purposes. These chapters are being written primarily to call attention to the precarious plight of the southern Negro and in an effort to prevent the tremendous injustices which he will suffer as a member of the Negro race and as a citizen of the southern States if the integrationists have their way.

The decision of the Supreme Court of the United States in the so-called "segregation" cases, Brown, *et al. vs.* Board of Education of Topeka, *et al.*, 347 U.S. 483, struck the South with the blinding impact of a hydrogen-bomb explosion. Stunned by this awful impact, the South, as a whole, and the clearheaded thinking people all over this great nation who knew that something was awry but did not know what to do about it, stood aghast, silent and apathetic, like an innocent man who had been convicted of a crime which had never been committed. Seizing upon this stunned silence, the proponents of integration saw an opportunity to gain the propaganda initiative, which they immediately did. "Experts" in the North and East, who are quite evidently unfamiliar with the racial problems in the South, immediately loosed a barrage of calumny against all who honestly felt that the Supreme Court was in error; against all who felt that the people in each locality and in each State were far better qualified to solve their own racial and local problems than were the inter-meddlers, regardless of how good might be their intentions but who knew nothing about the problem.

Many politicians, for reasons of political pressure and expediency, immediately seized upon the pretext of this decision for launching tirades of invective against the opponents of integration. Misguided reformers and designing agitators requested—and some of them "demanded"—the use, by the federal government, of the bayonets of the soldiery to enforce an absolute and complete compliance with the philosophy of the Supreme Court before the ink on the opinion was dry. We shall turn later to the political aspect of this matter and to the reason for its significance.

Much of the northern and eastern press seized upon the so-called "segregation" issue. Much space was devoted to a warped and distorted misrepresentation of the facts. Many radio commentators seized upon this opportunity to moralize and editorialize upon a subject with which they were sadly unfamiliar. Daily and hourly, by the radio and T.V., American ears were assailed with stories of the terrible racial strife in the South, of the South's unyielding discrimination against the Negro, and of *praise for the Supreme Court decision which they probably had never read and certainly did not understand.*

The decision itself rarely was quoted, and perhaps never appeared in full in public print. Its glaring weaknesses could not be recognized by the public if it remained unavailable for general reading.

A minority of newspaper, radio, and T.V. commentators adhered to straight reporting and factual discussion, admonishing the people to think clearly, act wisely, and practice moderation and tolerance.

Meanwhile, the *Daily Worker,* the communist propaganda sheet in the U.S.A., chortled in glee. The Supreme Court of the United States had cited as authority for its opinion in a most important case, the textbook writings of individuals, several of whom had been branded as left-wing sympathizers by members of the legislative department of the federal government. Constitutional and well reasoned precedent had been supplanted by sociological theory. The prospect of civil strife was imminent. At last the all-powerful Superstate appeared to be swallowing State and local government in the United States.

Although the decision of the Supreme Court to which reference has been made, was handed down on May 17, 1954, no complete and factual statement has as yet appeared to refute this mass of propaganda. Much has been said by political and civic leaders of the South and by many true representatives of the Negro race in the South, but little of this has seen its way into print and even less has found its way into the other media of public distribution of news. An objective and factual discussion of the entire matter will help to set this issue in its proper perspective and may contribute to its ultimate solution.

WHAT ARE THE ISSUES?

Shortly we shall strip the mask from the imps who feed the flames, and then we shall analyze the fuel they are stoking in such abundance. But first, let us see what the real issues are; and if they are obscure, let us bring them into the bright sunlight where they can be better examined. Let us examine them not only in the sunlight of today's knowledge but against the background of their true history, which can neither be disregarded nor erased. The issue has been falsely stated many times to be "segregation." According to the dictionaries, segregation means: "separation from others; a parting; a dispersion." As applied to relations among the races, it has been manifest throughout the world in the establishment in cities and congested areas of "ghettoes." The more modern meaning of segregation in the United States is the separation of the living quarters of races on a more or less voluntary basis, dictated not so much by difference in race as by difference in standards of living, places of employment, and the natural, understandable, and completely wholesome desire of each to be with his own kind.

Segregation is practiced just as effectively in Harlem, in the City of New York, in the South Side of Chicago, and generally throughout the North and East as it is in the South. One who has traveled through the Negro sections of the great cities of the North and Midwest will have observed that about the only difference in the segregation of the races as far as living quarters are concerned, whether it be East, West, North, or South, is the larger number of Negroes proportionately in the South. Segregation, which occurs in all sections of the country with or without laws upon the subject, is not the issue.

21

Neither is the issue one of equal protection of law, as we shall later show. The issue involved is not the denying to the Negro the constitutional rights guaranteed to him by the Constitution of the United States. The South may be reluctant to admit it, but in some sections of the South the right of the Negro to vote and engage in government as a citizen thereof has been withheld or slowly and grudgingly granted. Neither has the Negro in the past had the educational opportunities which would qualify him for such citizenship. However, these mistakes have to a great extent been recognized and within recent years great effort has been made, and is being made, to rectify them. This effort is being made not by the federal government but by the States, counties, and cities upon a local basis, which is as it should be. The discussion of the issue of forced integration in public schools therefore should not be confused by the interjection of other and distinctly different issues.

The problem created by the decision of the Supreme Court in the Brown case, and associated cases, *is devoted solely to the matter of the integration by force of white children and Negro children into the same schools in the South*—which schools are supported by taxation from the local government and not from federal funds.

Since most of the northern, eastern, and far-western states, many of whom have little or no Negro population outside of the large cities, have already decreed and practiced (at least to a limited degree) the integration of races in their public schools, this decision of the United States Supreme Court must be considered where it is applicable. Since it is applicable only in the South, it should be considered from the point of view of the South and in the light of the history of the South. The question, when stripped from all its pretences, should be stated thus, "Does the federal government, under the Constitution of the United States, through a decision of the Supreme Court of the United States, have a legal right to force the States of the South to require that Negroes and whites attend the same public schools without

regard to race? If the federal government exercises this alleged right, without specific constitutional authority, would
it be morally right?" These are the principal issues.

Two other major issues immediately are apparent, and
these should be borne constantly in mind in discussing integration. These issues are so momentous as to make one realize that they actually dwarf the forced-integration issue.
The first of these issues is the practical question as to what
effect the Court's decision, if enforced, would have upon the
southern Negro for whose benefit it was ostensibly made,
based on the theory he was an oppressed segment of the
citizenry of the country.

The other issue, and one which has been apparently ignored, may well be stated thus, "If the federal courts, under
the Brown *vs.* Topeka Board of Education decision, can assume jurisdiction in litigation involving the attendance of
students in a public school in a southern state, what would
be the circumstances under which federal courts could not
assume jurisdiction?" Is every case to become a "federal
case"? Are the restraints upon federal power as expressed
in the Tenth Amendment to be discarded? If every litigated
case becomes a "federal case," what would then happen to
the right of the people in lower-income groups, whether
white or Negro; and what would happen to local government, town, city, parish, county, district or State? Any
lawyer who practices in federal court must shudder when he
tries to answer this question.

CAN WE QUESTION THE COURT'S POSITION?

The overwhelming majority of southern lawyers and judges who have publicly discussed the Supreme Court's opinion are emphatic in their conclusion that it violates the Tenth Amendment to the Constitution of the United States. Evidently this argument is well founded, because apologists of the Supreme Court seek to justify its decision by saying that the Fourteenth Amendment, by implication, repeals the Tenth Amendment. Such arguments demonstrate the weakness of the decision. The Constitution itself provides the only method of amendment or repeal. The dangerous doctrine of constitutional repeal by implication has no place in our jurisprudence.

The proponents of integration, armed with this Supreme Court's decision, have suddenly blossomed into avenging angels bent upon a mission of establishing the sanctity of the Supreme Court and chastising any who would murmur a dissent. For three-quarters of a century they had assailed the courts of this land, particularly the Supreme Court of the United States, which had wisely and prudently ignored their imprecations and denied the use of the Supreme Court as a sounding board for their strange and misguided beliefs. Throughout this time, the Supreme Court of the United States had consistently ruled, in a great number of cases where the "equal protection of the law" provision of the Fourteenth Amendment was invoked, that the various States could not under any guise deny any person the equal protection of the law because of his race or color. It had held that no State could deny him the rights guaranteed under the Constitution—that is, the right to be a citizen of the country; to exercise the elective franchise; to acquire prop-

24

erty; to hold public office; to be tried by a jury of his peers; and to have equal standing in all the courts of the land with his fellow citizens. That Court has repeatedly held that a conviction for crime will not be allowed to stand in a case wherein a Negro is the defendant if, in that jurisdiction, his race is denied the equal protection of law by systematic exclusion from jury service. The right of the Negro to engage in the economy of his country and of his locality has also been uniformly upheld by the Supreme Court. These rights, plus the right to counsel, to a fair and speedy trial, to require witnesses to appear and testify in his defense, and to stand equal before the law, constituted "equal protection."

It had never before been considered judicially that "equal protection" meant that the races would be forced to play golf together, swim in the same swimming pool, live in the same housing projects, or attend the same schools. In fact, the Supreme Court had repeatedly held to the contrary in the matter of public schools. Both races in the South—or at least the vast majority of both—have, for almost a century, accepted the separation of the races socially, in schools and in recreation, as a normal and desirable way of life.

The Supreme Court has repeatedly refused to intervene in State or local matters where not authorized to do so by the Constitution of the United States. That Court, for almost a century, has consistently held that the Constitution did not authorize federal intervention in matters of a local nature which came under the reservation of the Tenth Amendment. This is probably as good place as any to point out that nowhere in that sacred document is the federal government given the slightest control over, nor jurisdiction in, matters pertaining to local school systems in any State or locality. The proponents of integration, however, and the agitators who desired to keep the racial question burning, have been before that Court many times in unsuccessful efforts to have it reverse its stand on this matter.

One important case was that of Plessy *vs.* Ferguson, 163 U.S. 537, decided on May 18, 1896, to which we shall refer at great length in the chapter devoted to that subject. That decision was against the integrationists and against those who now applaud the decisions of the latest Supreme Court. Time and time again these same people have assaulted the battlements of the Supreme Court in a vain effort to convince that Court that it was in error in the Plessy *vs.* Ferguson case and they have decried that opinion from one end of the earth to the other, challenging it as being unjust, unfair, and unconstitutional. Having assailed for so long the law as declared by the Constitution and as expressed by the Supreme Court of the United States, it is strange indeed to hear these same voices suddenly defend, with the greatest vigor, the infallibility of that Court as presently constituted. They apply such terms as "nullification," "defiance of the Supreme Court," "destroyers of the Constitution," "revolutionists," and many other similar but undeserved criticisms to those people who honestly and sincerely, and with a great abundance of legal authority, insist that the latest holding of the United States Supreme Court is erroneous and does violence to the very Constitution which that Court is sworn to uphold and defend.

In other words, as long as the Constitution was interpreted by the Court contrary to their wishes, the integrationists had no hesitancy in attacking the law as declared by the Court; but having a decision, at long last, in their favor, they now savagely insist that it is wrong in principle for anyone who disagrees with them even to question that decision. This appears to be a classic example that what is sauce for the goose is not sauce for the gander.

In furtherance of the propaganda program great effort has been made to have it falsely appear that, once the Supreme Court of the United States has spoken upon any subject, it immediately becomes the unqualified law of the land, and anybody who challenges the holding is disloyal and actually guilty of treason. Such, of course, is not the case. The Supreme Court is neither omnipotent nor infallible. Its decisions must be able to withstand all legal objections.

In the first place, the Supreme Court of the United States has no jurisdiction to pass upon a question unless that authority is specifically granted by the Constitution of the United States or specifically authorized by some constitutional federal statute. Generally we speak of a question which is subject to decision of the federal courts as being a "federal question." That means that it is a question involving:

Amounts in controversy in excess of $3,000, between citizens of different States or arising under the constitution, laws or treaties of the United States,

Admiralty, maritime, bankruptcy, or interstate commerce,

Patents, Indian Affairs, eminent domain by the federal government,

Postal matters, custom duties, internal revenue and matters arising from the operations of the federal government and other cases specifically provided for by federal statute.

It should be borne in mind that federal courts have no jurisdiction, except as specifically authorized by the Constitution and specified by federal law.

Contrary to political statements, and apparently public belief, the Supreme Court of the United States is not the supreme law of the land nor is it the supreme court of the land. Its authority is supreme only in those matters in which by law, under the Constitution, it has authority. The courts of last resort of the several States are the supreme authorities in those States and upon questions wherein the federal courts do not have jurisdiction.

The Supreme Court of the United States and the courts of last resort of the several States are, as all lawyers know, appellate courts. That is, they hear appeals from trial courts or intermediate courts of appeal. Ordinarily, a case in federal court originates in the district court; and if the judgment of that court is appealed, then it is tried on appeal in the United States circuit court of that circuit. There are ten judicial circuits in the United States, and these various courts are not always in accord in their decisions. Appeals

from these courts go by petition to the Supreme Court of
the United States. The final decision of the court, if it de-
cides to hear the case upon petition, is binding upon the circuit courts and the trial courts or district courts.

However, that does not mean the decision of the United
States Supreme Court is inflexible or that its decisions cannot be challenged or questioned. That Court is composed of
men just as are other courts. All men are subject to error.
All courts are subject to error, and as long as the democratic
processes continue, the decisions of all courts must be open
for inspection and subject to analysis to determine if they
are sound and in keeping with the fundamental law of the
land. To hold that the decisions of the Supreme Court of the
United States could not be questioned would invest that
Court with power that the Constitution never intended.

Petitions to rehear, arguing energetically, yet respectfully,
that the court of last resort had committed some error in the
case then under consideration, is not an unusual experience
for lawyers. That is almost a universal practice. Of course,
courts usually overrule petitions to rehear, but when the
same issue is raised again in a subsequent suit, it is common
practice for lawyers to appeal to the next court, or the next
term of the same court, for a reversal of a former holding
of that, or a former court, on grounds believed to be good
and in keeping with the basic and fundamental law. It is
not, therefore, wrong, nor is it unusual, to question the cor-
rectness of a court decision. In fact, the courts themselves
very frequently make such a challenge.

It is not at all unusual for courts of last resort completely
to reverse the decision in some former case and decide a
lawsuit then before them exactly opposite to the way it had
been decided by a previous court and sometimes even at a
previous term of the same court. Perhaps one of the greatest
tributes that could be paid to the courts of our land throughout the years of their political existence is that the courts
have not been reluctant to hear criticism of their opinions,
to consider arguments against them, and to reverse them

when it was clearly demonstrated that such opinions were erroneous under the law or under the facts. For the reasons later discussed, *the decision of the Supreme Court of the United States in the case of Brown vs. The Board of Education of Topeka, et al., is wrong and should be challenged in the American way in a forthright and respectful manner and by every legal means available.*

A failure to make this challenge, and to make it again and again, until it succeeds, will encourage and stimulate the abandonment of constitutional government in these United States as we have known it since the birth of the nation. In this case, it may well be said that *it is disloyal and unpatriotic to fail to make this challenge against a declaration of law which is not supported by the Constitution and would not be justified by a consideration of the true facts.*

A FRANK DISCUSSION OF HISTORICAL FACTS

Before analyzing in a legal way the decision of the Supreme Court, let us give some consideration to the moral side of the issue and to the factual discussion of the various issues involved.

One of the tragic features of the unfortunate integration issue, and the many years of agitation that preceded it, is the fact that many fine citizens of this country, who are law abiding, well educated, kindhearted, genteel people, but who have no personal knowledge of the facts, have been so flooded with propaganda on only one side of these issues that they have a completely distorted and untrue picture of the situation. Consequently, they are prepared to, and do, accept the spoken and oft printed words of the agitator, little realizing that they are doing themselves and their country the gravest injustice. *They have swallowed propaganda without noticing that it has no flavor of truth.*

We Americans are too often prone to accept as true, without question, the written word. In this age, with its tabloid newspapers, its automobile radios, and its millions of home television receivers, it has become almost a natural habit to let someone else do our thinking for us.

Another of our habits is the championing of anything labeled a "liberal" or humanitarian cause. We sometimes pride ourselves that this attitude constitutes "pulling for the underdog." Our schools, colleges, and universities have been particularly susceptive to these weaknesses. In truth, they constitute a serious malady if not accompanied by a full understanding of facts. Misinformation as to the historical and moral, as well as the legal, aspects of integration has become widespread. The only known cure for this malady

30

consists in large doses of the truth taken at frequent intervals with an open mind.

A good illustration of the far-reaching effects of this misinformation is found in an account of an actual experience of a southern lawyer in Mankato, Blue Earth County, Minnesota, in 1940. This lawyer, with a group of Minnesota lawyers and business men, was lunching in the Elks Club restaurant when the subject of racial strife in the South was introduced in a question by a young Minnesota lawyer. This startling question addressed to the Southerner was: "How many Negroes have you seen hanging from trees or telephone poles in your home town?"

The southern lawyer, of course, replied that he had never beheld such a spectacle and that, so far as he knew, the lynching of Negroes in the South simply did not occur; that the propaganda dealing with abuses of the southern Negro had little or no foundation in fact. In the ensuing conversation, several interesting and peculiar facts emerged. A number of those present had been greatly influenced by a deluge of propaganda to the effect that Negroes in the South were frequently lynched and hanged without cause and without trial; that Negroes in the South were mistreated physically and denied all other rights and privileges of citizens. The list of alleged abuses of the southern Negro by the whites of the South was practically endless, according to their information.

One still mysterious development was that these fine and intelligent citizens of a progressive city of 18,000 population, with one part-time Negro resident, were constantly deluged with this misinformation by way of the radio, newspapers, and public speeches without number. It was contained in the textbooks and taught to the children from kindergarten through college. As far as the visitor could distinguish, this propaganda did not admit to any change in conditions in the South since slavery days, or at least since the days of reconstruction. It seemed that no new material had been added and no change in conditions in the South recognized since the abolitionists had whipped northerners into a frenzy on the question of human slavery as it existed prior to the Civil War.

These business and professional men, none of whom had had any personal knowledge of, or contact with, conditions in the South, were extremely amazed and pleased to hear a southern lawyer discuss the great progress that had been made in interracial relations in the South in recent years. Perhaps the most difficult thing for them to grasp was the fact that the two races had learned, and were learning, to live side by side in peaceful coexistence, sharing economic and scientific progress and, at the same time, maintaining their separate institutions and cultures. Much propaganda has been directed to the theory that there can be no real progress in improving the lot of the southern Negro without removing all the restrictions, legal and moral, against intermarriage and social association. The last fifty years have demonstrated the fallacy of this argument as far as both races in the South are concerned.

A logical question arising in the minds of these Minnesota citizens was: "If these interracial conditions in the South are proceeding so satisfactorily, in the manner you have described, why do we have this continual barrage of propaganda to the contrary?" This is a good question, indeed, and one that should make all of us think.

In Seattle, Washington, in Rochester and Minneapolis, Minnesota, in Detroit, Michigan, in Ithaca, New York, in Caribou, Maine, in York, Pennsylvania, in Fresno, California, and in many other places, the same question has been asked. People who have asked this question—and their number has been legion—have been fine, upstanding, law-abiding citizens. They were not people who harbored hatred nor wanted to hold prejudiced opinions against any person, race, or sect of the country. They had heard this propaganda from the cradle to maturity. It had followed them in public schools, Sunday schools, religious meetings, social gatherings, and especially in political appeals. They had never heard the other side of the question. Many of them had not even supposed there was another side. These have not been isolated experiences. They fairly and accurately present a cross section of the feelings, information, confusion, and reactions of the public.

The agitators have apparently succeeded in making it appear to a great many American people that the southern Negro is demanding integration in the schools and that this propaganda is being carried on by him or in his behalf. This is not true. The truth is, and this should be repeated and reaffirmed until it is universally known, that the southern Negro is the one who will suffer the most from forced integration. *He is being exploited for political purposes and not for his benefit.* The agitation does not arise from the South, and the majority of the Negro leaders of the South are not in sympathy with the present program. They do not believe that it will be for the best interest of the Negro; and, in fact, they believe, and know, that he is the one who will suffer the most from it.

SOME OF THE REASONS FOR THIS AGITATION

There are three groups of people who are primarily responsible for, and who would expect to profit most from, a program of enforced integration in southern schools; or, to put it more truthfully, the publicity attendant upon such a program. These are: (1) The agitators, including the misguided; the reformers; the shysters who profit financially; and the lunatic fringe; all of whom converge upon any situation that can be made explosive. (2) The politician (not the statesman) hungry for the power of office; and the high-pressure groups and their leaders who would obtain political preferment by maintaining a balance of power in certain crucial border States of the Union. (3) The Comintern, the Cominform, or the international Communist party—whatever name it currently uses—which for many years has sponsored and encouraged the spreading of propaganda for the purpose of building up Communism through racial strife, civil commotion, and ill feeling.

It will be observed that there has been omitted from this list the vast majority of people of the North, East, and the Far West whose opinions have been molded from childhood by erroneous information, whose feelings and prejudices are built upon this incorrect information, and who, when they are acquainted with the true facts, will, in the American tradition, revise their thinking and join in an appeal for moderation, tolerance, reason, and intelligence.

It is not necessary to spend much time with the first-mentioned group. They are the claptraps, the fuzzy brains, the know-it-alls, the voodoo men, the "experts" upon every subject—and the greater their degree of ignorance, the greater their degree of expertness. They constitute the lunatic fringe. They hang on like camp followers to both major political parties and to every movement, both religious and sectarian. They are important only in that they become the carriers of political poison generated by more adept and cunning minds, and as often happens, their blatant arrogance enables them to deceive the unwary. *It is they who sing the hymn of hate.*

The second classification is far more dangerous, less numerous, and far more easily explained. Many of this class hold high positions. Some of them hold important offices in the State and federal governments; some only aspire to office. Many of them hope for political advantage for self or party, regardless of consequences; and many are simply victims of bad propaganda and poor information. This group would be greatly diminished if our electoral-college procedure were modernized so that designing politicians could not have so much to gain by appealing to minority groups in certain States.

Even now there is a movement underway to correct one of the great contributing factors to the confusion and propaganda. Under our electoral-college system, the candidate in a presidential election (or his slate of electors) receiving the majority of votes in any State receives the entire electoral vote for that State. For instance, in the great and often pivotal State of New York, with its forty-eight electoral votes, if the candidate of the Republican party received 2,500,001 votes and the Democrat candidate received 2,500,000 votes, the Republican candidate would carry the State and would receive all the electoral votes. The same condition, of course, exists in every State. It would be possible, by the bare majority of one vote in each of the States of New York, Pennsylvania, Illinois, Ohio, and California, for one party to win a landslide in the presidential election by obtaining, in additon to the States which are traditionally Democratic or Republican, these five great States by a majority of one vote in each. This could occur even though the winner actually received less than the majority of the popular vote. Of course, this is rather an extreme example, but it could happen, and it emphasizes our problem. As long as a few votes in any of these electorally powerful States can have such a tremendous effect on the outcome of an election, it means that any militant and organized minority which can control its voting members within any of those States has a political balance of power entirely disproportionate to the remainder of the population; and it is a balance of power which should never exist.

One of the great advocates of integration in the South is one Adam Clayton Powell, a Democratic Negro congressman from the Harlem District of New York City. Nobody could blame Mr. Powell for doing everything legal and reasonable within his power to serve the people of his district. But he was not elected by the Negroes of the South, and they are not looking to him for any redress. They do not even appreciate his efforts; and, in fact, many of them resent the fact that he is willing to make them victims of a great political, and possibly physical, bloodletting in order to give his district and his constituents from the State of New York a balance of power in voting in the national election—a power which the Negroes of the South and the white people of the South do not possess, and one which Mr. Powell's constituents should not possess. This example is typical of many others.

The danger, above referred to, has been recognized, and corrective measures are under way. There is now pending a proposed constitutional amendment, the exact terms of which are not yet definite, but which, if and when adopted by the several States, will provide in effect that the electoral votes from each State will be apportioned among the various candidates according to the popular vote of that State so that the vote of each citizen will count in the final tabulation of the electoral votes regardless of whether or not he was in the majority of his own State. By simply making this much needed change in our election machinery, we can abolish the power of much of the militant minority pressure groups and when that is done, the apostles of hate who have been exploiting the southern Negro for their own particular political benefits will suddenly lose all interest in him.

The third group agitating for enforced integration in southern schools is the Communist party. Its party newspaper in the United States, the *Daily Worker,* has been most active in trying to inflame hatreds and stir up jealousies between the races and between different sections of this nation. It has ridiculed and bemeaned every statesman who made a plea for the preservation of constitutional government. It has magnified racial differences. If it has not advocated outright violence, it has certainly advocated the creation of a condition in the South which everyone familiar with the situation realizes must inevitably end in violence. The purposes of the Communist are so insidious, so inherently dangerous to our free institutions and so detrimental to our way of life, that we should be critically suspicious of any cause which they espouse. In analysing their propaganda therefore, it is important not only to analyze what they are saying, but the underlying reasons for their saying it. Their ultimate objective is the important consideration. We shall discuss this subject hereafter under the title "What Do Communists Want?"

LO! THE POOR INDIAN

For the sake of argument, it may be admitted that many whose hearts bleed so profusely for the "poor southern Negro" are moved by genuine impulses and inaccurate information. On the other hand, many of these "bleeding hearts" are suspect for a very good reason. Their motives could be far more pure if they had a genuine interest in the truly downtrodden minorities of this country and of the world.

When the white man came to these shores, he found a fierce and proud race in possession of its great plains, its heavily wooded mountains, and its fabulous resources. The American Indian was the owner—in possession—of all this great wealth which the white man coveted. The Indian title thereto could not be questioned under any law, ancient or modern.

Through violence, bribery, deceit, broken promises, and the introduction of "firewater," the white man deprived this noble race of its heritage. The Indian was driven from his home, his hunting ground, and his cherished freedom, and, through military force, was chained to a "reservation," where he was made the ward of his conqueror. For the most part, these reservations were in arid and unproductive areas; and with the exception of a few tribes enriched by later discoveries of oil or some other resource, the economic plight of the Indian reached a deplorable state. Sickness and starvation decimated the survivors. The Indian was denied the right to vote in the government of the land which he had once owned. He was effectively barred from the industrial economy of the country.

If the placing of the Indian in reservations and keeping

him there by force does not constitute "segregation," then the term has lost its meaning. If these "bleeding hearts" really wanted to attack a problem of enforced and unjustified segregation, why have they not begun on the Indian problem? Since the day that the white man first made his appearance upon this continent, the plight of the Indian has grown steadily worse. Since the American Negro was first brought to this continent as a slave, his plight has grown slowly, but steadily, better. It is true that this growth has sometimes been painful, but it has always been toward an improved status.

The Indian, having no right to vote, has not been able to be used as a possible balance of power in a political campaign and, therefore, have the advantage which this country wrongfully gives to pressure groups. The Negro, in many instances, has had that advantage.

Both major political parties have given lip service to better treatment for the red man, but the promise and the performance have been halfhearted. There has been no such ardor and breast-beating as occur on behalf of the southern Negro—particularly in election years. The most recent development was a presidential directive issued by Mr. Eisenhower—or someone in his name—which seems to place the Indians' welfare upon a "local" basis. Is it not strange that the Indian, a ward (or prisoner) of the federal government, is a "local" problem, while the southern Negro, a citizen in his own right and in his own State, must be protected from local or State laws by federal decree?

Candidates for, or occupants of, federal offices must ever face the demagoguery of those individuals or groups who seek to grasp and use this balance of power. Naturally, the prime target is the President of the United States. Mr. Eisenhower is generally regarded as one of the great men of the age. He is a person of great renown. Even his political adversaries admit privately and publicly that there is no guile in the man and, while he may have been misinformed upon some domestic questions, that he always acted, and they believe will continue to act, with the highest degree of integrity.

Mr. Eisenhower has spent a great portion of his life in the military. He has had very little time to become acquainted with the South and its civilian problems. He could not have a firsthand knowledge of the actual problems that beset the South upon racial questions. He must take his information from the same sources as other comparative strangers to the South; except that, in addition, the presidential ear will be besieged by politically minded people more eager to carry the electoral vote in a certain State than they are to achieve justice or to insure the triumph of truth. A public figure traveling throughout the United States would hear only, and see only, those things which his managers, friends, and advisors desire him to see and hear. He would come in contact not with the ordinary run-of-the-mill citizen but with people representing pressure groups and organized endeavors.

Few will doubt that if Mr. Eisenhower had the opportunity to acquaint himself with the facts of the racial problem in the South, he would come up with an answer which would be just and satisfactory. As chief executive and head of one of the three branches of government, he must accept the decision of the Supreme Court in a particular case. He is not in the position of an ordinary citizen. That does not mean that he could not recognize the obvious error in the decision, nor does it mean that he would be restricted from counseling as to a proper solution to a problem aggravating a great section of the country whose chief executive he is. *He also must protect and defend the Constitution.* Some agitators have, within recent days, called upon the President to use the power of his office to supplement their conception of the Supreme Court's opinion and have even urged him to use force in beating down opposition to this opinion in the South.

We can be sure that the pressure placed upon the President by these high-pressure groups has been tremendous. Nevertheless, it is an encouraging indication that Mr. Eisenhower has such an innate sense of justice and rightness that, in spite of this political pressure, up to this time he has counseled moderation, tolerance, and a reasonable approach through local channels to the solution of this problem. He has such courage and integrity that, if he had the facts, he would divulge to the American people the true state of affairs, and suggest a solution legal in its nature, moderate in its tone, and efficient in its operation.

He has only to look about him in Washington, D.C. to observe the shambles of that city's schools as a direct result of forced integration. The wholesale exodus from our capital city to Maryland and especially to Virginia (where schools are segregated) is but a small sample of what we may expect if and when forced integration is attempted. Nor will such counter-measures be restricted to the southern or border states.

KILLING A FEW WEEDS

Uncle Lige, an old Negro man who had grown to manhood in slavery, was the handy man on a farm in southwest Virginia. He was too old to do heavy farm labor, so his chief activity consisted in telling stories to the white children. Uncle Lige had a lot of native wit and ingenuity, although he had no formal education and could not read or write. He had spent most of his life with, and working for, white people. His vivid imagination and his ability to tell stories made him a veritable Uncle Remus. His beaming smile and courtly dignity characterized an era which had known gracious living. Often he spoke in parables and with pungent wit.

One day, seeing a snake wriggle into a patch of high weeds, a boy who was listening to his stories seized a hoe and started to kill the snake. Uncle Lige pulled him back with a restraining hand and said: "Wait till I get my scythe and cut down dem briars and weeds. If you go atter him 'thout seein' whar yore gwine that snake might wrop hisself round you. If you wants to kill the snake stead of lettin' the snake kill you, we ud better do some weed-cuttin' fust."

Let us do a little weed-cutting. Maybe when all the brush is removed, there will not be any snakes to kill. If the people who have agitated for integration in the schools in the South and who have berated and bemeaned the South really knew the actual facts of the matter the size of our racial problem would be greatly reduced. It seems that those who would feed and fan the flames of our racial fire choose to ignore or disregard the statistics which show that: lynching in the South is virtually nonexistent; Negroes are treated better in the courts of the South than in other States; and that Negroes in the South are making great educational strides under the "separate but equal" facilities system.

One of the first steps to a solution of the racial questions in the South is to counter the false propaganda that has flooded this country and to supplant it with a true statement of conditions. This can be gleaned far more readily from personal observation and experience than by second-hand information or statistics, no matter how vivid.

This suggests a challenge and an invitation to the detractors of the South to come to some portion of the South and bring with them their propaganda, prejudices, and preconceived ideas about conditions here. This does not mean a political tour whereby some well-known or highly advertised public figure flits from State to State and is met at the airport with a handful of political puppets, pressure groups, and hangers-on, then whisked away to a banquet at which he is the principal speaker. Instead, he should live and work with the people of the South, both whites and Negroes, and take part in community activities, politics, schoolwork, and civic undertakings. After our visitor has been in this salubrious clime, if he has lived with anything like an open mind for a twelve-month period, he will go back to his native North or East a much wiser and happier traveler. He will say to his Yankee friends, "I have been wrong. I have agitated against the South. In my righteous indignation, I demanded that troops be sent to the South and that offenders be put to the bayonet for disagreeing with my views on the integration of white and Negro children in the schools of the South. I was unaware of the history of the South and the traditions that make up the thinking not only of the white people but of the Negroes of the South. I had been misinformed as to the treatment which the Negroes of the South received.

"I was not aware of the great advances he had made nor the great efforts being made by the southern States to provide the Negro with educational facilities for building himself into a real citizen of the South. I realize now that my method was wrong; the only method that can be followed with any success is the method of education, improvement, toleration, and understanding, which can only be developed with the passing of time. I realize now that the purposes which we thought we wanted to accomplish cannot be accomplished by judicial fiat or military force but only by the processes of democracy and of education."

A few years ago a very intelligent young man employed by one of the major oil companies related the following dramatic story of his awakening.

"I am a native of Connecticut, where I attended school and college, including several terms at Yale University. Although I was studying the sciences, I had some courses in sociology and was very active in public speaking. I had never been out of my native New England, but I was a true expert on racial problems, particularly the problems of the West Coast where the Asiatics and the Mexicans were concerned and of the Negro problem in the South. As a sophomore I gave the South hell for lynching, abusing, and mistreating the Negroes wholesale. I envisioned the land as a place where the Negro was not only helpless but completely innocent. I saw him being denied all of his constitutional, economic, and political rights. I envisioned him being lynched without trial, denied any participation in government, and his school facilities so meager as to leave him completely unable to compete with the white citizens. I had heard and read all these things, and if somebody had suggested raising an army to march upon the South to avenge the wrongs done to the Negro, I would have been the first to volunteer.

"Shortly before the beginning of World War II, I was sent to California by my employer, ready to do both my job in the oil industry and my duty as a citizen toward correcting the great injustices that were being inflicted upon the Asiatics and the Mexicans by the cruel whites of California. I had not been in California long before it slowly began to dawn upon me that maybe I was not a true expert and probably the people of California were far better able to cope with the problems with which they were thoroughly

familiar than I, who had only a second- or third-hand grasp
of the matter at best.

"I played golf every Sunday morning in a foursome upon
a course close to my home. There was a foursome of young
Japanese men who usually played just ahead of us. On Sunday, December 7, 1941, the day of the attack upon Pearl
Harbor, we gathered for our usual round of golf; and after
having played some two or three holes, someone remarked
that the Japanese foursome was not in evidence that morning. Neither, for that matter, were any other Japanese in
evidence. Thinking little of it at the time, we proceeded
with our game, which we finished in the late morning hours.
Just as we were preparing to leave the course, the news of
the Japanese attack upon Pearl Harbor came over the radio.

"One of the fellows with me, engaged in the same business, was a native of California. He said, 'This means trouble. I knew that there was something significant in the fact
that no Japanese appeared on the course this morning; let's
go to our properties immediately.'

"I did not know what he meant. We rushed to the field.
On some of the land leased by our company there were
large fields of growing crops. To my horror, I discovered
that on that Sunday morning many of these crops had been
greatly damaged or totally destroyed. Some of them had
been cut down and some plowed under. Great vineyards had
been destroyed; groves had been cut down; and damage
which you probably never heard of had been inflicted upon
property both public and private in the State of California.
Remember that this damage had been done before and
during the attack upon Pearl Harbor and before any an-
nouncement had been made of it.

"Shortly thereafter, I was sent to Louisiana, where I remained in the oil field for two years, living and working with
people of that region. I worked constantly with Negroes
and lived in a community where they outnumbered the
whites about three to one. I soon learned that all I had been
told about racial conditions in the South was completely

wrong. But, more important, I learned that all I had ever conceived as a solution for the so-called 'Negro problem' in the South was more wrong than my lack of knowledge about the problem itself.

"Instead of being something that can be solved overnight by passing a law or issuing some kingly decree, problems of the South relating to racial questions must be solved by education and tolerance. I realize now that in my full enthusiasm I was one of the world's biggest fools. From here on out, I propose to make my avocation the spreading of the truth as I have found it from personal experience."

Some of the weeds, therefore, that we should cut might be labeled "ignorance of the facts." Other weeds or briars that hide the snakes have either been planted there or carelessly dropped as seeds by the passing birds. One of the rankest of these growths is the fallacy that the South's resistance to the Supreme Court's decision on integration is based upon some theory of "white supremacy." As a matter of fact, the Supreme Court's opinion indicates most clearly that it was also based upon this fallacy.

So-called "white supremacy" was a factor in the South following the Civil War. Except in the minds of some southerners that term did not mean what is usually implied by its use. It is not necessary to try to hide or in any way conceal the stark realities of the past. They greatly influence the present and cast their shadows toward the future.

It should be stated categorically that the argument against integration of the schools in the South is not predicated upon this Civil War philosophy of white supremacy. Separate facilities for white children and Negro children do not imply that one race is superior to the other. The fact that races are different and have different histories, backgrounds, inherent characteristics, ambitions, standards of living, personalities, and ambitions does not render one race superior and the other race inferior. It may be that the most active and ambitious races are the ones who have caused the most trouble in the world.

There is nothing in the world more natural than the old adage that birds of a feather flock together. Color of plumage may be different, but the different color, size, or shape of the feather does not imply that one type of bird is better than, or superior to, another. Indeed one may well conceive that a Rhode Island hen, authoress of our national breakfast food, possesses the greatest beauty because of her utility and that she is superior to all of our other feathered friends. Another may, with good reason, favor the peacock, with its royal plumage. Some think that no bird surpasses our native quail or bobwhite. However, we should find no fault with someone who sincerely believes the golden-throated canary or the lyrical-voiced mocking bird is "better" than the quarreling bluejay or the parrot given to mimicry. It is natural for birds, beasts, and humans to separate each according to its kind. It does not mean that they cannot live and work together in the same country and in the same political system nor that they cannot engage together in the same fields of commerce, industry, and agriculture.

The Negro of the South does not want to be forced into integrated schools in the South any more than white people of the South want the same thing. He knows that people work better, live better, learn better, and act better in the relaxed company of their own people than they do in the artificial atmosphere of enforced *co-mingling*.

Shortly after the Supreme Court's decision was announced, a group of representative Negroes went to members of the Board of Education of Greene County, Tennessee with this plaintive inquiry: "We have heard of the Supreme Court's decision and we don't understand it, but we would like to know if this means that we have to give up our Negro schools?"

They were assured that such was not the case. However, that assurance was probably prematurely given. If sanity is not restored to this question, and if the completely erroneous decision of the Supreme Court is carried to its ultimate conclusion, it would certainly mean that those Negroes would have to give up their schools. A great many agitators either overlook or purposely ignore what everybody in the South must recognize to be the truth, and that is that enforced segregation would in reality do the Negro of the South far greater harm than good. It would hurt him much worse than it would hurt the whites. It would rob him of many of the gains that he has made and would destroy—and in fact is now destroying—the fine and friendly relation between the races in the South which had been growing apace within the past quarter of a century.

No full understanding of the problem may be had, no proper appraisal thereof can be made, in the absence of some knowledge of the history and the deep-seated traditions involved in this question in the South.

In the not-so-civil war between the Union and the Confederacy, the South was fighting for a cause which it believed to be holy and just. It could not be denied, of course, that many people of the South fought because they wanted to preserve the institution of slavery and to keep from losing the economic advantage that they enjoyed in life by virtue of owning slaves.

Others, however, and this included the real heart of the Confederate cause, built around men of the character of Robert E. Lee and "Stonewall" Jackson, believed that in matters not specifically delegated by the Constitution of the United States, as expressed in the Tenth Amendment, that the rights of the States to local government was and should forever remain supreme. It is true that they lost the war, that the institution of slavery was abolished, and the Thirteenth, Fourteenth, and Fifteenth Amendments to the Constitution of the United States were enacted. But it cannot be seriously contended that any of these subsequent amendments repealed the Tenth. If so, it is strange that such repeal was not discovered by any court or government for nearly a century.

A LITTLE CONSTITUTIONAL STUDY

It will be recalled that when the Constitution of the United States was presented to the States for ratification that there was much fear that an enactment of the Constitution into the fundamental law of the land would give the federal government, or the central government, too much power. Accordingly, the first ten amendments, known as the Bill of Rights, were proposed by Congress to the legislatures of the several States on September 25, 1789, and were ratified by all the States, except Connecticut, Georgia, and Massachusetts, before the end of the year of 1791, and thereby became a part of the Constitution.

Unfortunately, many people who prate about constitutional privileges have never taken the time and trouble to study the Constitution. Perhaps reference to that great document would serve as the scythe that we need to cut down more of the weeds. The amendments to the Constitution which comprise the Bill of Rights provided in substance as follows:

1. Religious and political freedom.
2. The rights of the States to keep militia and the right of people to bear arms.
3. Prohibited quartering soldiers in homes.
4. Prohibited unreasonable searches without a proper warrant.
5. Provided for a grand jury in felony cases; prohibited double prosecution for the same offense; provided that no person should be required to give testimony against himself nor be deprived of life, liberty, or property without due process of law.

6. Protected the right of the accused in criminal cases so as to guarantee a fair and impartial trial.
7. Provided for the right of trial by jury.
8. Prohibited excessive bail and cruel and unusual punishment.

The Ninth and Tenth Amendments are so important that we quote them verbatim:

9. "The enumeration in the Constitution of certain rights shall not be construed to deny or disparage others retained by the people."

10. *"The powers not delegated to the United States by the Constitution, nor prohibited by it to the States, are reserved to the States respectively, or to the people."*

So provided the Bill of Rights.

The Eleventh Amendment (1798) was designed to preserve the sovereign independence of the States by prohibiting suits before the federal judiciary against any State by citizens of another State or foreign state.

One wonders why this amendment has not been invoked to prevent the multitude of suits against the southern States, usually in the name of some pawn or figurehead, but actually by the N.A.A.C.P.

The Twelfth Amendment (1804) enlarges or explains Article 2 of the Constitution, with reference to the election of the President and Vice-President.

This electoral system, good 150 years ago, is archaic and obsolete in this day of universal suffrage, rapid transportation, and instantaneous communication. Its modernization would help to eliminate many evils of high-pressure minority-bloc politics.

The Sixteenth Amendment authorizes the Congress to pass income taxes.

The Seventeenth Amendment relates to the election of

senators, United States senators, by the people.

The Eighteenth Amendment, the prohibition amendment, gave the federal government the power to regulate or prohibit the manufacture, sale, and use of intoxicating beverages.

The Nineteenth Amendment gave women the right to vote.

The Twentieth Amendment changed the date of the terms of office of the President, Vice-President, and members of Congress.

The Twenty-first Amendment repealed the Eighteenth Amendment.

The Thirteenth, Fourteenth, and Fifteenth Amendments to the Constitution, insofar as they could possibly refer either directly or indirectly to the subject under discussion, provide as follows:

> Amendment 13. "Neither slavery nor involuntary servitude, except as a punishment for crime whereof the party shall have been duly convicted, shall exist within the United States, or any place subject to their jurisdiction."
>
> Amendment 14. "All persons born or naturalized in the United States, and subject to the jurisdiction thereof, are citizens of the United States and of the State wherein they reside. No State shall make or enforce any law which shall abridge the privileges or immunities of citizens of the United States, nor shall any State deprive any person of life, liberty, or property without due process of law, nor deny to any person within its jurisdiction the equal protection of the laws."
>
> Amendment 15. "The right of the citizens of the United States to vote shall not be denied or abridged by the United States or by any State on account of race, color, or previous condition of servitude."

It is clear from the foregoing that there is no constitutional provision clothing the federal government with the power to regulate State or local schools nor is there any delegation of authority to exercise authority or jurisdiction over the schools. The Constitution in Article 3 is very specific in detailing powers granted to the federal government and very specific, in Amendments Nine and Ten, in what is reserved to the States and to the people. *Until the Supreme Court, in its recent opinion, held to the contrary, no decision of that Court, no State or federal law, and no provision of the Constitution of the United States had ever given the federal government the right to control local schools.* It is true that for many years the proponents of enforced integration upon the South have held out as bait to taxpayers and voters the illusion of federal aid to the schools in order to enter the back door and put the federal government in control of the schools. But this effort has been stoutly resisted and defeated.

In spite of these facts, however, which are well known and unassailable, a great many people in this great land of ours have been duped into thinking that the Constitution of the United States required white children and Negro children to go to school to the same schools; and that, by having separate schools for the two races, that the South was actually violating the fundamental law of the land and denying to the southern Negro his "constitutional" rights. The purely legal nature of this matter will be discussed in a later chapter; but to have a reasonably intelligent approach to the problem—if indeed it is a problem—these provisions of the Constitution and the reasons behind them should be borne in mind. As every student of constitutional law knows, the Supreme Court of the United States has consistently held for many years that the Fourteenth Amendment did not prohibit the States from passing laws providing for separate schools for the white and Negro races.

THE HISTORIC PERSPECTIVE

Following the Civil War, the South found itself in a state of great confusion and degradation. Its cause was lost, its governments demolished, its currency debased, its economy wrecked, and its sovereignty impaired. Its population of defeated and bankrupt whites was almost engulfed by a flood of freed slaves who were also impoverished, without education, with little training for citizenship, and ill equipped to adjust to their new freedom. Defeat, death, and desperation kindled in the minds of the southern whites the flames of hatred for their late enemies. These flames were fanned by the advent of the carpetbagger from the North.

This is a chapter in our national history of which none of us can be proud, but one which must be recognized when dealing with the problem which it helped to create. These carpetbaggers did not represent the philosophy of the great, but martyred, Lincoln, nor did they have the blessing of his successor, "The Tennessean," Andrew Johnson. They were political vultures who descended upon a land weak almost unto death from one of the most vicious bloodlettings the world had up until that time endured. They took charge of the economy and of the government of a great part of the South. They dealt out not justice but vengeance. Negroes who had recently been slaves, and who were untrained, uneducated, and completely unequipped for such tasks, were elevated to public office. They occupied governor's mansions and State houses. They were "elected" to the legislatures. In a short space of time, they became the masters of those whom they had formerly served as slaves. Unwittingly, they were made to serve the pernicious purposes of the carpetbaggers and were used as the instrument to punish further and degrade the southern whites. It is not our purpose here, and there is not the space, to describe this revolting episode in our history. Those who are unacquainted with it, or who find it interesting, can find volumes upon volumes in any public library.

Bitterness between the white and Negro races, which up until that time, even through the Civil War, had been practically nonexistent, suddenly flared into a major conflagration. The State governments sank to an unbelievable low. Law and order practically fled. Pandemonium reigned, and the bitterness engendered by the War between the States was as nothing compared to that brought about by its aftermath. The whites, greatly outnumbered, were the objects of persecution. Rape of white women by Negroes was prevalent. It was useless to call upon any established agency of law for protection. Under these conditions, unusual events transpired. Bands of night-riders or "white caps" soon sprang up. The "Invisible Empire" of the Ku Klux Klan came into being, and through these illegal but effective methods of spreading fear into the hearts of newly freed Negroes, some semblance of law and order was gradually restored to the South. It should be borne in mind in reviewing the history that those were days that truly tried men's souls. Passions ran rampant. Cool and mature deliberation was hardly possible. A great cooling-off time was necessary before reason could be restored. We must admit to our shame that the victorous Union forces of the North gave but scant help to their restoration.

The next chapter is one of which the South cannot be especially proud. Nevertheless, it was a natural consequence of all that had gone before and, to a certain extent, could not have been avoided. It was apparent that the Negro, although the shackles of slavery had been stricken from his limbs, had not been trained mentally, emotionally, or morally either to operate government or to participate therein. A proper system of education for the Negro, if begun at that time, would have solved all our problems ere now. That is much easier to say in retrospect than it would have been to perform in those days. It should be fairly admitted that, on the part of many southerners, there was still too much bitterness prevalent to permit any desire to educate or improve the Negro, either intellectually, morally, or economically.

However, an even stronger reason prevailed. The economy of the South had been practically destroyed. It had few factories and depended largely upon agriculture. Its methods of transportation were crude and slow, to say the least. The financial and political centers of the nation were at that time almost exclusively in the East. As railroads were built to replace the much slower water traffic, freight rates were so discriminatory against the South as to make it difficult, if not impossible, for it to ship the products of its fields and forests to the North and East in competition with the rapidly growing Midwest.

Under these adverse economic conditions, there simply was not enough money or credit available to enter upon a program of education for the great number of whites and Negroes who needed it so badly. As a matter of fact, we are likely to forget that in those days, education, as we now know it, was hardly a matter of public concern. Schools were few and mostly private. There was no compulsory education, and it might be truthfully said that many of the white, and none of the Negro, children for decades following the Civil War had even a tenth of the educational opportunity now available in the South to all persons.

Having but little educational opportunities and many times less encouragement from the better educated and more fortunately situated whites, the Negro for a short while made very slow progress as a race. Nevertheless, many of the individual members of that race made phenomenal progress. Negro schools sprang up, sponsored by local or religious groups and later by the expanding educational systems of the several States. Men like George Washington Carver appeared on the horizon to give great leadership and inspiration to the Negro race. Gradually, as the States moved into a system of compulsory and universal education, agitation appeared among the people of the South for greater facilities for Negro education. At first these facilities were very meager and, to be truthful, poorly attended. Many Negroes did not see the need of, or enjoy the prospect of, an education. The more ambitious felt that they had been deprived, or were being deprived, of some of their rights or privileges as citizens and sought to equip themselves better and to participate in the government and the affairs of the States. But these efforts were resisted.

The great body of the Negro citizenry in the deep South was, and still is, not adequately prepared to participate as fully as they should as citizens in the affairs of the State and Nation. The fact that they have been slow in this regard is, of course, due to the fact, in many instances, that they have not had the educational facilities which they require. It will be pointed out by many southerners that the Negro, having but little property, made little or no contribution in the way of taxes in support of schools until the passage of the sales-tax law which spread that burden upon all people. There is truth, of course, in this statement, which we must recognize. Nevertheless, when the Negro was made a citizen by the Constitution of the United States, and when the laws of the several States required education as a compulsory thing, it became the duty of the States to see that the Negro had facilities for education. Slowly, as this realization dawned and the economic conditions of the South permitted, these facilities began to be made available.

Although the decision of the Supreme Court discounted such statements and, in fact, admitted that the lack of facilities was not a consideration in its opinion, the propagandists have continued to insist that the major reason, or one of the major reasons, that they have pressed for integration in the South is that the Negroes do not have educational facilities and they must go to school with the whites in order to obtain them.

MORE WEED-CUTTING

This would probably be an excellent place to do some more weed-cutting. The truth is that in many localities of the South the Negroes have better school facilities than the whites. Some States have not yet caught up, but they are catching up rapidly. Recently the State of Alabama completed a multimillion-dollar school-building program. Approximately seventy per cent of these facilities were devoted to colored schools. The State of Georgia had a seventy-million-dollar building program—largely Negro schools. The State of Mississippi is now initiating its greatest school-building program in history, and it is practically all devoted to the building of schools for the Negroes. In a great many cities and towns of several of the southern States, the finest, newest, and best equipped school buildings are those that have recently been completed or are now under completion for Negroes. This is necessarily true because the white schools were built first, and they are older in architecture, in design, and in equipment.

Recently, the writer had the opportunity of visiting with local people in a number of cities, towns, and communities in Georgia, Alabama, Louisiana, and Mississippi. One city visited was La Grange, Georgia. La Grange is a city of 30,000 population, and while figures are not exact as to the division between colored and white, the Negro population is equal to, or exceeds, the white population. Needless to say, the white children were in schools for the white, and the Negro children were in the Negro schools. They appeared to be quite happy about the arrangement and not in the least frustrated. In the Negro

58

schools there were more modern and better facilities than those occupied by the whites.

Still other weeds of rank growth are those concerned with spreading and keeping alive the completely false illusions that: (1) The Negro is imposed upon and universally mistreated in the South; (2) this mistreatment extends to physical violence and frequent lynchings; and (3) the Negro does not receive justice in southern courts. The last libel is sometimes stated: "There are two kinds of court justice in the South—one for Negroes and one for whites." The inference is that the constitutional prohibitions contained in the Eighth Amendment against cruel and inhuman punishments were generally disregarded in the case of the southern Negro. Not one of these weeds deserves to live.

Having consideration for the history of the South since the Civil War, it may be impossible for non-southerners to realize that conditions are as peaceable as they now are. Our nonresident friends think and talk of conditions which existed several generations ago and which have become ancient history to the South. Stories of abuse of southern Negroes are so fanciful and farfetched they would be amusing except for the sad fact that so many uninformed people believe them. Talk privately to any southern Negro, and 99 times out of 100 he or she will deny being mistreated. Furthermore, it is better than an even bet that if he has been working in the North or East, he will say that he is treated better in the South than elsewhere.

No intelligent person would claim perfection in the South, or elsewhere, in interracial relations. Yet it is doubtful if history records any instance where two races as diametrically opposed in color, temperament, heredity, and history as the southern whites and Negroes have accomplished, in so short a time, such a peaceful coexistence. It is a tribute to both races. It was accomplished not because of, but in spite of, outside interference.

Lynching has become very rare in the South. When it

existed, it claimed persons of both races, as it did in other parts of the nation. Indians, Mexicans, and whites were summarily tried and hanged—or just hanged—for many alleged crimes, but usually for stealing cattle or horses. There were very few Negroes in those areas at that time. Cattle-rustling and horse-thievery subsided as law and order was established. We hear no derogatory or inflammatory tirades against present-day westerners because some of their immediate ancestors either condoned, or participated in, lynching. In truth, there is a State park and museum at Langtry, Texas, which is a memorial to Judge Roy Bean— "the law west of the Pecos." An attendant points out the shank of a tree where alleged horse thieves were hanged after a summary trial in the saloon. There was no appeal.

One crime that always aroused southern men to a frenzy of hatred and vengeance was the rape (and usually murder) of a white girl or woman by a Negro. The great majority of Negroes deprecated this crime as much as the whites did, and they endeavored to eliminate it. Following the Civil War, when southern law enforcement reached a low ebb and the Negro found himself the possessor of a freedom with no training in self-restraint, rape of white women was a frequent occurrence. Considering the fact that there were about three million Negroes in the South, it is obvious that only a very small percentage of them committed the crime of rape, and, likewise, a comparatively few white people committed the crime of lynching. When law and order was re-established, the crimes of rape and lynching subsided. The oratory castigating the South has not subsided.

To the eternal credit of the southern Negro and to the eternal shame of his exploiters, it must be confessed that the reign of terror which accompanied "reconstruction" days was not instigated by the Negro, nor by the southern whites. It came upon the crest of exploitation and vengeance that surged over the South like a tidal wave at the end of the Civil War. Then, as now, the unrest, tension, and ill feeling between the races in the South was engendered by persons from the outside for reasons that were anything but altruistic.

The true conditions existing during the period of "reconstruction" were well known to the public men of that day.

Henry W. Grady was an outstanding public figure of this period. In 1886, he penned the following significant passage: "We remember with what fidelity for four years he guarded our defenseless women and children, whose husbands and fathers were fighting against his freedom. To his eternal credit be it said that whenever he struck a blow for his own liberty he fought in open battle, and when at last he raised his black and humble hands that the shackles might be struck off, those hands were innocent of wrong against his helpless charges, and worthy to be taken in loving grasp by every man who honors loyalty and devotion. Ruffians have maltreated him, rascals have misled him, philanthropists established a bank for him, but the South, with the North, protests against injustice to this simple and sincere people. *To liberty and enfranchisement is as far as law can carry the Negro. The rest must be left to conscience and common sense. It should be left to those among whom his lot is cast, with whom he is indissolubly connected, and whose prosperity depends upon their possessing his intelligent sympathy and confidence.* Faith has been kept with him in spite of calumnious assertions to the contrary by those who assume to speak for us or by frank opponents. Faith will be kept with him in the future, if the South holds her reason and integrity."

Perhaps the best proof of the statement that the southern Negro is not mistreated by the South is found in the statistics concerning arrests and punishment for criminal violations. It may be partially true that there are two systems of justice in southern courts; but if so, the Negro gets the better of it.

The following is copied from the *Congressional Record* (Vol. 102, No. 54, Page 5093) of March 27, 1956: "It should be noted that the integrated States show a substantially higher incidence of Negro crime in proportion to Negro population than the segregated States. In fact, this table (contained in the *Record*) reveals that the percapita crime rate among Negroes in the integrated States is 199 per cent—or double—the rate in the segregated States. The cases enumerated in the foregoing table are convicted felony cases, and the figures do not reflect arrests or misdemeanor convictions.

"These figures must prove conclusively one or two premises: Either that Negroes are more law abiding in a segregated society, or that southern courts are far more lenient with Negro defendants. This, in my opinion, puts the lie to the left-wing and N.A.A.C.P. propaganda to the effect that a "reign of terror" against Negroes prevails in the South.

"Much of the propaganda assault made against the southern people originates in the State of New York. To those from that State who would criticize the South, I suggest a look at the record.

"In 1950, New York courts sent more Negroes to the penitentiary than the courts of Arkansas, Mississippi, and South Carolina combined, in spite of the fact that the total Negro population of those three States exceeds that of New York by 1,317,019.

"According to the 1950 census, Mississippi's Negro population exceeds New York's Negro population by 68,303. Yet, official Justice Department figures show that New York sent twice as many Negroes to prison in 1950 as Mississippi.

"Where is the reign of terror, if such exists?

"Integrated Ohio sent more Negroes to prison in 1950 than did the segregated States of Arkansas, Tennessee, and South Carolina combined. Those three southern states, according to the 1950 census, have a Negro population that exceeds that of Ohio by 1,266,247.

"Again—where is the reign of terror, if such exists?

"The foregoing figures will show the startling fact that the integrated States sent more Negroes to the penitentiary in proportion to their over-all Negro population than the segregated States. Per 100,000 Negro population, this rate ranges, in the northern States, from 77 in Pennsylvania to 386 in Maryland. By contrast, the rate in the segregated southern states ranges from 22 in South Carolina to 128 in Virginia. . . .

"It should be noted that the white prison rate per 100,000 white population is practically the same in all the States reported, being 21 in the integrated States and 29 in the segregated States.

"These 1950 figures, further analyzed, show the following:

"On a per-capita basis, New York sent 9 times as many Negroes to the penitentiary as whites; Pennsylvania sent 8½ times as many Negroes to prison as whites.

"New Jersey's population is 7 per cent Negro, but 35 per cent of their felony convictions were Negro. In other words, 7 per cent of their population was responsible for 35 per cent of their major crimes.

"The same pattern holds true practically throughout the integrated States.

"Among the southern States, South Carolina actually sent more whites than Negroes to prison on a per-capita basis. On the basis of 100,000 population by race, South Carolina sent 145 per cent more whites than Negroes to prison. This is the only State in the Union, according to available statistics, where this condition prevailed."

All of the foregoing quotation is copied from the *Congressional Record*.

WEEDS THAT MASQUERADE AS FLOWERS

Obviously, it would be impossible even briefly to mention all of the untruths, half-truths, and misunderstandings which we have referred to as "weeds" and which confuse the issues involved in the question of racial integration in the schools. It would be well, however, to notice a few more of these weeds that pretend to be fragrant blossoms. They can usually be recognized as high-sounding phrases, snappy slogans, or vague generalities which signify nothing. Among these terms we find such fancy specimens as "constitutional liberalism," "civil rights," and "second-class citizens." These terms and others, which can be interpreted in a multitude of ways to suit the convenience of the user, frequently appear as the false premises upon which integrationists base their spurious arguments.

"Constitutional liberalism" is a frequently used term which seems to have some strange fascination for so-called "liberals" or intellectuals. The term "liberal" is purely a relative term. That which may appear as "liberal" to one person or group may seem strongly conservative or even "reactionary" to some; while to others it may have all the earmarks of radical socialism. The term "liberalism," when applied to the Constitution of the United States, and when reduced to plain language, simply means an interpretation of the Constitution, regardless of its plain terms, made to suit the desires of the user or the political needs of the moment. It is "stretching the blanket" to the desired shape and size without consideration for what may happen to it.

The Constitution of the United States was written in simple, forthright language by intelligent and farseeing

64

patriots who were founding a new way of life. They did not engage in double talk. They drafted and redrafted the Constitution until it was recognized and ratified as a solemn contract among the several States. The terms of this contract, as all contracts, must be interpreted according to the usual, ordinary, and generally accepted definition of the terms as they were understood by the contracting parties.

These terms have been interpreted by the courts and accepted by the States and the people, in the manner stated, since the creation of the Constitution and the various amendments. If the basic meaning of a contract can be changed one hundred years after it is made by the simple expedient of redefining its terms, then such contract has no validity. The advocates of "constitutional liberalism" are saying in effect: "We realize the Constitution does not support our position, so we are going to change the Constitution by 'liberally' construing it. We recognize that this amounts to an amendment to the Constitution and that such amendment is not made in the manner provided in the Constitution." If this solemn contract can be twisted and distorted by interpretation, then we may as well have no written Constitution. The Constitution clearly provides the method of amendment.

Another stratagem employed by the integrationist is to include their scheme of social and scholastic integration by force under the general phrase "civil rights." The civil rights guaranteed by the Constitution of the United States and the laws and constitutions of the several States should not be denied to any citizen. The term "civil rights" is clearly defined in the Constitution and statutes. Its meaning has been known and accepted by the States and the people for a long period of time. It may well be true that some States and localities have deprived the Negro of some of his civil rights on the basis of color. Such abuse, if and when it existed, could not justify the extension of the meaning of civil rights to include a forced mixture of the races in schools, in marriage, or in social intercourse.

Another weed which is often said to have the fragrance of a rose, but which actually has only its thorns, is best described by the catch phrase, "second-class citizen." This phrase is most usually used by political speakers or exhorters, and its greatest effectiveness seems to be achieved when the speaker, rising to great heights of offended dignity, declares in loud tones: "We do not have, and cannot have any second-class citizens in this great nation."

This statement overlooks the undeniable truth that we do have second-class citizens, as well as third-and-fourth and possibly lower-class citizens.

The different classifications of citizenship are not, and should not be, based upon color, race, or religion.

A first-class citizen is one who honors his country's laws, contributes to its economy, schools himself in the obligations and duties of citizenship, and fully discharges those obligations.

A second-class citizen could be defined as one who lives within the law, but who knows and cares little about his country's history, who has no concept of government, who never qualifies himself to perform any of the duties of citizenship, and whose only contribution consists in growling about what others have done.

There is another class of citizen who not only fit the description of second-class citizens but, in addition, have so little regard for their country and its institutions of freedom that they permit others to use them to defeat those very freedoms. There are many citizens of this country, of both races, who do not vote, or if they do vote, engage in what is known as "bloc voting." Could it be seriously insisted that a citizen is "first-class" if he meekly submits to the political domination of some so-called labor "leader" or local "committee" and votes as he is instructed to vote without regard to the issue involved or the merits of the respective candidates? It could hardly be denied that the big political machines of the cities many times remain in power through this method of voting.

It is undeniably true that, in several localities in the South, the Negro vote is delivered as a unit, or practically so, by a "leader" or a "committee" who deal with the prospective candidates and unquestionably profit therefrom.

A criminal does not lose his citizenship because he is a criminal. He may, in certain instances, be deprived of the elective franchise and the right to hold any office of public trust, but even the confirmed criminal, if a citizen of this country, still remains one. Do the orators want us to believe that such a citizen is "first class"?

Instead of being a valid argument, these catch phrases are simply propaganda antics designed, at least in part, to confuse the issue and to make the Negro think that he is getting something for nothing. If this can be accomplished, he may not realize until it is too late that he is being exploited in a cause that will do him far more harm than good.

WHAT DOES THE SOUTHERN NEGRO
STAND TO LOSE?

It might be well to pause and consider briefly just what the Negro has to lose by enforced integration in southern schools. We used the term "enforced integration" because that is just what is implied in the present situation. Integration may, and probably will, eventually come to the South and all over the United States. But that will occur sometime in the future when the whites and Negroes are ready intellectually and morally for integration. The southern Negro will eventually assume that place in society, in finance, in government, and in schools which by virtue of his ability, character, educational qualifications, and his integrity he is entitled to assume and hold. No judicial fiat, threat of legal action, no amount of agitation, no bloody bayonets can hasten that day by as much as one hour or one minute. It is quite conceivable that violent and ill-advised action might retard or delay that day, but it can never hasten it.

When, by education, tolerant understanding, and democratic processes, integration on a voluntary basis is accepted in the South and in the United States, it will have long since ceased to be an issue. When that time comes, it will not be desired save in a comparatively few situations. Negro children, when necessary, or more convenient, may go to white schools; white children under the same circumstances may go to Negro schools. If the facilities they require are not otherwise available, particularly in the college or graduate schools, both races will probably attend the same schools without a thought as to race. But, as that day approaches, the desire of the Negro to be with

68

his own kind, and the desire of the white to be with his own kind, will continue to manifest itself as a law of nature. When given the opportunity to attend mixed schools, the majority of the members of both races in the South will reject it in favor of attending the schools of their own people. As a matter of fact, that is their present attitude and will continue to be their attitude.

What are some of the losses the southern Negro would suffer by an enforced integration in the schools at this time?

First, he would lose the exclusive right to use the fine buildings and equipment which have been made, and are being made, for his own benefit.

Second, he would certainly lose, to a great extent, the right and privilege of going to school with members of his own race and to teachers of his own race. At least for many years to come, the school boards of the South will be composed of white people. And whether one likes it or not, it is still an undeniable fact that they will elect white teachers to operate the schools. They can do this largely on the basis of qualifications, either real or superficial. Many Negro teachers would become unemployed. This would be a serious setback.

Third, the Negro would be denied his place of leadership. In his own schools and own organizations, as well as in his own church, the Negro must supply his own leadership and authority. This training in leadership is indispensable to continued progress of the Negro race.

Fourth, when placed in integrated schools, the majority of Negro students would not be able to keep pace with their white classmates. The result would be truly one of frustration and defeat. This may sound like a manifestation of what the agitators call "white supremacy." It is nothing of the kind. This thought comes not from the writer, nor from any prejudiced source, but from talking to the mothers of the little Negro children who are now in school. Any person who wants to establish the same facts can do so by going to the private citizen or any Negro mother in the South, talk freely to them, and ask their opinion about it.

This is their feeling. They do not want their children to go to school with the white children. They do not believe that it would be for their best interests in any respect. They point out that their children would not be as well dressed, would not have the same standard of living, would not be interested in the same things as the white children; and even if no trouble ensued between the races, that the Negro children would be handicapped and pushed to a place in the rear and would suffer from a feeling of inferiority and frustration.

Going to school with the white children will not raise the Negro's standard of living nor put any more money in his pockets. The writer has not yet talked with a mother of a Negro child who has not earnestly and sincerely insisted that all she wanted was a good school for her child to attend and that her child would be far better off going to a Negro school than going to a mixed school.

Fifth, the Negro would also lose the pride and accomplishment that come from having his own institutions. Many people do not know that in the South there are many Negro schools and educational institutions which are not part of the public-school systems but which are supported in whole or in part by State or public funds.

Stillman Institute is a Negro institution in Tuscaloosa, Alabama which is supported at least in part by State funds. When the Autherine Lucy incident arose (we shall deal later with that deplorable occasion), a member of the legislature of the State of Alabama announced that he would introduce legislation to deprive this great Negro school of its State appropriation. It may be argued that such an attitude is wrong, but argument would not restore the appropriation. It is a fact which must be recognized and is probably typical of what may be expected over a wide area of the South.

It must be borne in mind that the southerner—and this is not restricted to the members of the white race—does not believe that segregation is wrong in the public schools, nor is he convinced, even by the Supreme Court decision to the contrary, that he is, or has been, guilty of doing anything wrong in providing excellent and adequate separate facilities for educational purposes.

Sixth, the southern Negro will lose by the disruption of that friendly progress which has been going on in the South during recent years between the races. A survey has recently been conducted among newspaper men and many other leaders in the South inquiring whether or not conditions between the races in the South have changed as a result of the Court decision and the efforts toward integration. Almost without exception these men have said that tension had grown up between the races and that there was considerable evidence of a slackening of good feeling and a foreboding of trouble. We shall refer to some of these statements later.

This increased tension and slackening of tolerant understanding between the races will hurt the southern Negro not only educationally and politically, but it will in many instances be a severe blow to him economically. In many sections of the South, the work of a southern Negro is confined almost exclusively to agriculture. In most instances, he does not own the farm upon which he works, but is a hired hand, a tenant, or sharecropper. Generally, his employer, either a white man or corporation, furnishes him a place to live, tools with which to work, and, in a great many instances, finances him in advance so that he can buy the necessities of life for himself and his family.

Whether he lives in the city, in a small town, or in the country, the southern Negro needs credit. Generally, he must obtain this credit from white people. He borrows his money from a white man at the bank or the loan company. More often than not he obtains credit from the white owner of the grocery store or clothing store. With few exceptions, the man or firm selling him his automobile is white. A white man arranges his insurance and finances the partial payments on his automobile or his household furniture.

When he or his family becomes ill, the southern Negro, unless he lives in a city, is cared for by a white doctor. Many times he does not have immediately available the money to pay the doctor, and the doctor credits him. This list could be extended almost indefinitely. It requires no unusual perception to realize that when friction arises between the races, when the seeds of hatred are sown by people for the purposes which we have discussed, then the southern Negro will find himself less and less able to obtain credit, to obtain work, to receive the consideration and understanding without which many times he would not be able to make ends meet. This is not a threat. It is an actuality which even now is taking shape in many places in the South. Whether it is right or wrong is not the question at the moment. Rather, the question is: Is it a reality?

Very recently a streetcar, or bus, boycott by Negroes in Montgomery, Alabama received great play by many newspapers and news commentators. A few local agitators, with much outside encouragement, tried very energetically to whip up an incident of racial strife. The strike began as an alleged protest against segregation of the races on city buses, in accordance with Alabama law. However, the agitators soon expanded their efforts to include all segregation of the races. This is one of the few instances in which outside agitators have succeeded in obtaining a local Negro spokesman. Many Montgomery Negroes are not enthusiastic about the strike. Many of them realize that, if they win, they will still lose much and gain little. Meanwhile, those without an automobile or means of transportation either walk or do not get to work.

It is comparatively easy for the well-paid—and well-cushioned—attorneys and agitators of the N.A.A.C.P. (which is usually referred to in the South as the "National Association for the *Agitation* of Colored People") to ride around through Harlem or some northern city in a Cadillac and advise the southern Negro to walk rather than to ride, as he has been doing for decades, in segregated buses. The question immediately involved is not whether it is morally or legally right to have segregation upon the public buses in the City of Montgomery or in public schools or golf courses. Our consideration is whether or not such agitation by outsiders, in an obvious effort through strikes, boycotts, civil commotion and their unrelenting efforts to force upon the white people of the South something they are not willing to receive, does more harm than good to the Negroes of the South.

It is not easy for the southern Negro—nor for anyone else under similar circumstances—completely to turn his back upon or attack those who claim to be his champion. The agitators try to make the southern Negro think that if he does not line up with the N.A.A.C.P. or if he does not join in their activities that he is disloyal to his race. Comparatively few Negroes believe it, but some of them do. Even if they do not subscribe to the N.A.A.C.P. doctrine, it is embarrassing and difficult for them to take the lead in opposing these agitators who are ostensibly trying to help them. If the southern white people will get together and say to the present-day carpetbaggers, "GET OUT!" the great majority of Negroes of the South will join their white brethren, even as a great many of their leaders have already done.

Seventh, this program of forced integration appears to be designed to destroy the pride of the southern Negro in his race. Throughout recorded history one of the finest and greatest motivating forces of any people has been pride of blood, race, and family. Each race has its own characteristics, hopes, and aspirations perpetuated in song and story. The southern Negro is no exception. As a race of people, he is distinct from any other on earth. When he has the opportunity and training, he has a sunny disposition, a spirit of fairness and of loyalty unequaled anywhere. He learns rapidly and is a great competitor. He is musical to an astonishing degree. Normally, he is the happiest individual on earth. The integrationists would destroy all these fine characteristics and set the Negro about a task of trying to be something he is not and trying not to be something that he is.

Much music was built around the southern Negro, and some of the finest folk songs of the South are either about Negroes or designed to be sung by Negroes. Who is not thrilled by the lyrical beauty of "My Old Kentucky Home" or "Old Folks at Home," with their talk of "darkies" and their melodious sentiment? "Dixie," which was not originally a southern song but a song to be sung by Negroes, is what might be aptly termed the national anthem of the South. The Negro spirituals hold a unique place in the folk music of the world. It has been said that these songs are the Negroes greatest contribution to America's culture, and America's greatest contribution to music.

Jerome Kern, in composing music for *Show Boat,* wrote a Negro song which has become something of a teething ring for amateur bassos the world over. This is the reverberating and melodious song "Old Man River." As every schoolboy knows, that song starts out: "Niggers all work on the Mississippi, Niggers all work while the white folks play . . . you don't dast make the white boss frown."

Within the last few years, whenever this song has been sung in public places or on the radio, the rich phraseology of the author has been altered so that, in effect, the words declare: "People all work on the Mississippi, people all work while the rich folks play . . . you don't dast make the big boss frown." This silly and childish alteration robs the song of its original meaning and substitutes a series of meaningless phrases.

We can safely assume that the southern Negro was not responsible for this change; more likely some trouble-maker on the lunatic fringe started promoting the idea that this fine old song was a reflection upon the Negro race; or, even more likely, he or she wanted to leave that impression for the purpose of creating the ill will and tension which such characters have at last begun to build up in the South. The changing of the words in the song is unimportant in itself, but it is simply an indication of how little the trouble-makers really know about the Negroes of the South and the southern people. The Negro of the South cannot be changed into something that he is not by changing the words, phrases, or references in literature.

His *record* of accomplishments against handicaps in the last ninety years in the fields of music, economics, athletics, and citizenship has been so good that it is not necessary for him to pose as something he is not. *Nothing can be accomplished by making him a nameless and faceless figure ashamed of his own race and his own people.*

One of the greatest wrongs which these inter-meddlers—which we also call "integrationists"—have perpetrated, and are perpetrating, against the southern Negro is to make him appear simply as "comrade citizen" and to deprive him of all his individuality.

WHAT WOULD EVERYBODY LOSE
BY ENFORCED INTEGRATION?

We have analyzed briefly what the southern Negro would lose by enforced integration in the public schools in the South, but let us now consider what everybody would lose and what some of the dire effects might be. No segment of the citizenry of any country or any section of a country can suffer serious setbacks without affecting every other segment. These prospective losses are facts, not fancy. They cannot be disregarded nor ignored. They should be faced fully and frankly, and it is necessary to face them to gain any understanding of the moral issues involved and to determine whether the decision of the Supreme Court is morally right or wrong.

The first and greatest loss we would suffer by enforced integration in public schools would be a legal as well as a moral loss. That is the loss of the guarantee of the Tenth Amendment to the Constitution of the United States that the powers not delegated to the federal government are reserved to the States. *It cannot be repeated too often, and the Supreme Court's decision cannot be challenged too sharply, that the Tenth Amendment to the Constitution stands squarely across the path of integration as decreed by the Supreme Court.* It cannot be overemphasized that the Constitution nowhere gives to the federal government the right to control public schools, and no amount of subtle sophistry can change or alter that fact.

If the Tenth Amendment means what it says, and what the Supreme Court of the United States and all other Courts have said that it meant for over a century, then the latest decision of the Supreme Court on the question of

76

integration is flatly in the face of, and in violation of, that provision. The Supreme Court reversed a former decision of its own, one made with different personnel, when it reversed the case of Plessy *vs.* Ferguson, which was decided in 1898. But the important fact is that the Supreme Court cannot reverse the Constitution of the United States. If the Tenth Amendment means nothing and if it can be violated, rescinded, repealed, ignored, or overridden by any authority whatsoever, then all the States have forever lost their sovereignty.

There has been a tendency within recent years to run to Washington with hands outstretched, begging for this gift or that grant, as if the federal government had some large secret cache of cash from which it could dole out favors. In order to accept or get into position for accepting these grants or favors, the several States, their governing bodies, and citizens have been content, or at least willing, to surrender one bit of State sovereignty after another to gain the illusory benefits of these federal grants which, in fact, are nothing more than a return to the people of the several States a portion of money taken from them by way of taxes. The remainder, of course, is lost in the gigantically expensive and bureaucratic business of big government. This eagerness on the part of many of the States and State officials to get what appears to be "something for nothing" has given aid and comfort to those who would increase the debts and extend the authority of a central government even in violation of constitutional prohibition.

The loss of State sovereignty means the loss of right to local government. Our forefathers who established this great country and ordained its form of government were very fearful that they would create a Frankenstein monster which would devour the very principle of liberty which they and their fathers had fought so hard to obtain. They wanted a central government strong enough to provide for the national defense, to protect the member States from enemies without, to assist in the development of the great undeveloped portion of our country, and to assist in the carrying on of trade and commerce. But they did not want a central government so strong as the deprive the individual of his liberties and of his right to control himself through local governments created by him through representatives elected by his ballot. The very essence of personal liberty, as opposed to the autocracy of a totalitarian state, is the right of the individual to create and to maintain local government sensitive to the wishes of the majority of the people in that locality. The Constitution laid down broad principles which the States could not transgress but left up to them the solution of all local problems.

The loss of the right to local self-government through the destruction of the Tenth Amendment is a price much too high to pay for any advantages, real or imaginary, which the integrationists in their wildest dreams might promise. If the people of Connecticut or Montana, for instance, seriously considered what it would mean to their local self-government if the Tenth Amendment were stricken down by this decision of the Supreme Court, they surely would also rise in arms and say, "We must not destroy our Constitution!"

EVERY CASE A FEDERAL QUESTION

Another price which we shall all have to pay if, by the establishment of enforced integration, the Tenth Amendment to the Constitution is abolished and the authority of the Supreme Court of the United States over our schools is accepted, is the loss of individual rights and freedoms through the protection of our local courts. A loss of the right of self-government, under the guarantee of the Tenth Amendment, and the loss of individual rights and liberties through the making of every question a "federal question," far overshadow any other issues involved in the late decisions of the Supreme Court.

Traditionally the federal courts have exercised only a limited jurisdiction, which was granted to them under the Constitution of the United States. Suits between or among citizens of different States of the Union; suits by or among the several States; suits or indictments for crimes arising in the exercise of federal functions or upon federal property; maritime suits; suits involving the federal government or the functions thereof; and suits invoking the question of constitutional right under the Constitution of the United States comprise a large backlog of litigation in the federal courts. Cases which may be taken into federal courts are referred to generally as "federal questions."

Questions which are not federal questions are necessarily limited or restricted to trial in the courts of the various States. Municipal courts, county courts, circuit courts, and State courts abound in number throughout the land. Although some of their dockets are crowded, particularly in the large cities, generally a citizen who is charged with a crime or who has a wrong which he believes should be righted can obtain a reasonably speedy trial in the courts

79

of the several States. It would not be true to say that
these trials are always speedy or that they are always
economical, but—and this is the most important feature—
generally they are far more speedy and far more economical than suits in the federal courts.

It is not merely that our federal trial courts are more
expensive to the litigant, who must often travel much
longer distances to go to court; nor is it most important
that the trial of his suit may be delayed more in most of
the federal courts than in the State courts. The procedure
in the courts is entirely different. In many respects the
power of the United States district-court judge is almost
unlimited. The United States district judge can almost tell
the jury what verdict to return. He has the authority, in
some cases, to release one convicted of crime on bail
pending his appeal or to send him on to jail while his
appeal winds its tortuous and expensive way through the
federal appellate procedure.

Many of the federal trial courts are now crowded beyond
belief. Trials are months and, in some instances, years
behind the filing of the case. (An appeal from the United
States district court to the court of appeals, to be followed
perhaps by a petition to the United States Supreme Court,
is an expensive procedure.) Unless the losing party in
federal court has substantial funds or has the support of
some high-pressure group well heeled with funds from
some strange source, he can ill afford—in fact, cannot afford
—the cost of an appeal.

Think what would happen to the average individual if
all cases brought in court were federal cases and could be
filed in, or removed to, federal court. Persons, firms, or
corporations with great financial backing, with a retinue
of capable, retained lawyers, would, of course, not hesitate to put all their cases in federal court, particularly
if they were not in a hurry to try them. But the poor individual, the average citizen, the wage-earner, the tenant
farmer could not afford this luxury. It could be said

honestly and factually that if every legal question in this country became a federal question, then the legal and civil rights of the great majority of the common people of this country would be almost extinguished or made so expensive to defend as to be denied.

This is not an indictment of federal trial courts either as to the laws under which they operate or the very excellent gentlemen who serve as judges thereof. As a general rule, lawyers enjoy the practice in federal court and enjoy appearing before the federal judges. (However, they realize that it is a different type of court from the State courts, that the laws, rules, and regulations there are different. They would all be forced to agree that if a great percentage of cases now tried in the State courts were suddenly dumped into the federal courts of this land that their dockets would be so hopelessly clogged that an entire army of new federal judges and federal courts, together with their attendants, would have to be created.)

Even if new federal courts were created, duplicating the personnel of the State courts, the difference in the federal procedure and the difference in costs and appeals in federal cases would still deprive the poor citizens of this country of a fair and impartial trial in a local tribunal before a jury of their peers and a trial which they could afford. One must indeed shudder to consider the dire effects that would follow upon making every legal question a federal question.

One of the greatest sufferers, of course, would be the southern Negro. He is the most numerous of all those people who can ill afford to have their cases tried in federal courts. Let's face the question squarely. Whether the Negro children in La Grange, Georgia attend only the fine schools constructed there for the Negroes and the white children there attend only the white schools operated as schools for white children, rather than schools mixed as to race, is a federal question, *then what is not a federal question?*

The Supreme Court, in its swift dash to destroy local

government and establish a federal judicial dictatorship, has invaded local schools, local street buses, State universities, city police departments, city parks, municipal golf courses, public recreation, local and intrastate commerce. *Having jumped the restraining fence of the Tenth Amendment, where will the new restraining fence be found?* Or have we abandoned restraint of the federal judiciary? Since its unconstitutional but autocratic power is now felt on the golf courses, in swimming pools, and even in the kindergarten, how will this all-powerful Court be denied access to all private business and recreation? We may expect its mandates to regulate bridge parties, family picnics, and even enter into the sacred precincts of the family circle.

Are not the two losses which we have mentioned too great a price to pay for integration of the southern schools? Or do the proponents of integration care about the price we must pay? To be more explicit, are they interested in the price which the South must pay directly and the entire nation indirectly? Or, are they interested in creating strife, disunion, commotion, tension, bitterness, and perhaps violence for their own or for subversive reasons?

ANOTHER DANGER TO OUR ECONOMY

Mention has been made of some of the many ways in which the southern Negro would suffer economically from enforced integration in the schools. He will also suffer as a citizen of the southern States from the financial debacle which would likely follow such enforced integration. The language of money is one that people generally understand. There is no method of measuring the value of principle in terms of the dollar. But when a principle is violated and is accompanied by the prospects of great financial losses, it is doubly deplorable.

The southern States which will be affected by integration have within the past decade built hundreds of millions of dollars worth of schools. Most of them have been schools for the Negroes. These States, of course, did not have cash on hand to pay for this tremendous building program and had to borrow money by the sale of bonds. These bonds, issued for the construction of new school facilities in the sum of hundreds of millions of dollars, are now owned by banks, trust companies, insurance companies, and investment accounts all over the country. The ability to pay the principal and interest on this huge indebtedness depends upon the collection of taxes by the various States, counties, and municipalities in accordance with the terms of these bonds. An empty schoolhouse, however new, would be worth little or nothing to bondholders.

Some of the southern States, and likely a majority of them, resent any effort on the part of the federal government to run the State schools. They feel that the federal government has no valid right to take such action, and they will resist it to the utmost. Any effective step which they may take to resist this federal encroachment will likely result in a failure to pay school bonds and the interest thereon. Any step in this direction would very likely affect the financial standing of the municipalities involved to the extent of destroying their ability to issue new bonds for other purposes or, perhaps, cause a default in the payment of other bonds.

The implications of the financial angle in this matter are far-reaching indeed. Such a financial catastrophe as we have envisioned would not only hurt the South, but its disastrous effects would be felt in the money markets of the nation.

The prospect of the default in hundreds of millions of dollars in municipal bonds is not an idle speculation. Several States have already enacted laws which, in effect, would close their public schools if there were an attempt to force integration by federal power. The State of Georgia, for instance, has passed a number of such laws. It is not only possible but quite probable that the public schools of several southern States would cease to be public schools the minute an effort were made to force a mixing of the races in the schools. It is also quite probable that when this occurs defaults will also occur on many State, county, and municipal school bonds.

The likelihood of financial default and of the deterioration of fiscal properties, though of tremendous importance, is as nothing compared to the deterioration of the scholastic standards which will inevitably follow forced integration in southern schools. There is much evidence that the recent integration in the schools in the District of Columbia has not only resulted in lower scholastic standards for all schools but in a great exodus of white people from the nation's capital to nearby States having segregated schools. Such lowering of standards is admitted by all who are familiar with the situation to be an inescapable result if integration is forced upon the southern States. The question arises:

Why force upon an unwilling section of the country an illegal, unconstitutional, and immoral philosophy that will do such awesome damage to its fiscal, physical, and scholastic accomplishments?

INTERMIXTURE OF THE RACES

Many of the States of the Union and many of the southern States have either laws or constitutional provisions prohibiting miscegenation. Marriages between persons of different color are positively prohibited. Intermarriage of the races is regarded by both races not only as unlawful but as undesirable and repugnant to nature.

If there has ever arisen from any southern Negro or any group of Negroes in the South a demand for intermarriage or relaxation of the rule against miscegenation, it has not been made public. They recognize, as do the whites, that it is much better to maintain the purity of each race than to encourage intermixture of the races, with the consequent grief that it brings.

We read of intermarriage of races in the North and East occasionally, and if they want to indulge that habit, it is no business of the southerner; but he does not want them to try to enforce that habit upon the South. It may be that a very limited number of Negroes, or whites, in the South would be interested in intermarriage, but the percentage would be so small as to be negligible. *The laws against miscegenation are simply the legal expression of a way of life accepted by both races as desirable and the product of experience.* Such indeed is the basis of all established law.

One may well ask what integration has to do with intermarriage. In *Miami Life* of Saturday, March 17, 1956, appeared the following:

> As fast as one facet of the problem is smoothed down, another—even more grating upon the emotions—comes to life.
>
> The intermarriage question, for instance. The

National Association for Advancement for Colored People, you know, has said intermarriage is a natural consequence of integration—and that is their ultimate goal.

Intermarriage has been practiced, at least to a limited extent, in some sections of the United States. Any discussion as to the success or failure of such marriages of the races is better left to local experience. Neither race in the South wants intermarriage in the South. The people of the southern States want to retain their constitutions and laws prohibiting intermarriage. This applies to both races. If they did not want to retain these provisions, they would repeal them. If they are repealed, the people of the southern States want to do their own repealing and not have it forced upon them by outsiders.

In spite of these undeniable truths, however, the proponents of integration have stated repeatedly that they will spare no effort to force integration upon the South. They proudly parade their belief that integration in the schools would naturally result in intermarriage between the races. The N.A.A.C.P. has announced through its officials that it was committed to a program of "full integration." This last term, as understood by the N.A.A.C.P., means integration in marriage, in social affairs, and in the family circle, as well as in schools.

On May 28, 1954, the *United States News and World Report* printed an interview with Walter White, executive secretary of this organization. Mr. White, who was reputed to be a Negro with a white wife, stoutly defended marriage between the white and Negro races. He contended that it was improper, immoral, and unchristian to prevent interracial marriage. As evidence of the intention of the N.A.A.C.P. to turn integration in the schools into a fight to remove all legal barriers against intermarriage, this official said: "The association of the races in public schools leads to friendship, love, and marriage."

These statements have been widely quoted, but as far as the writer knows, no person connected with this high-pressure group has ever denied them. If it were denied, the fact would still remain that intermarriage will sometimes occur as a consequence of integration. If children of tender age are placed in schools where integration is enforced by law, they, of course, must attend class together, sit together at school, play together at lunch or eat together in the cafeteria, ride together on the buses, and play together upon the playgrounds. Let us here omit any discussion as to the possible misunderstandings, quarrels, friction, strife, bitterness, and violence which will unquestionably attend much of such forced integration. Rather we will assume, for the purpose of argument, that the integrationists' dream can be carried off in a very orderly and pleasant manner.

If the two races associate in class, on the playground, in the cafeteria, on the buses, in the gymnasiums, and in the chapel, they would undoubtedly do so in the class parties and in plays given by the various classes. Social events given for a school or a class would necessarily include both races. If little Mary, with blue eyes and golden hair, is taught by her teachers (who, if forced integration comes, will be *de facto* federal employees) that all people are the same, that there is no difference between them but the color of their skins, that she should go to school with Negroes as well as the whites and associate with them in class, in the cafeteria, at play, and in social gatherings— then what is to keep little Mary from allowing little Johnny, with the dark eyes and the crinkly hair, to escort her home from one of those socials?

Let us suppose they linger a moment at the doorstep, breathing the perfume of wild honeysuckle, enthralled by the mocking bird's matchless mimicry, while the southern moon works its mystic spell. Will little Mary find any serious objection to Johnny kissing her good night? If courtship follows, either clandestine or otherwise, is there any reason why little Mary shouldn't marry Johnny? Southern parents of both races will think there is a very great reason.

Let us assume, however, that marriage does follow and that, in the normal course of events, children are born to this union. These children would be neither white nor Negro. They would represent the first stage of amalgamation of the two races, the first act of the breaking down of barriers which have protected the racial purity of the two races. Neither race would fully accept the offspring of intermarriage. For all practical purposes, in the South such children would be literally "without a country."

Integrationists may, of course, respond that the "law" establishes that there is no difference between the races; and when southerners recognize that it is proper for the white children and the Negro children to be required by federal law to go to school together that the problems will disappear. Such answers ignore the ethnic questions which have been recognized as tremendous factors in human behavior since the dawn of civilization. No amount of demagoguery or moralizing will destroy the opposition of southerners to miscegenation; neither can they solve the social and economic problems of the half-breeds. While their number may not be great for some time to come, their problems will be very great.

In all frankness, it must be considered that forced integration in southern schools will help to create, or greatly intensify, two interracial problems. These are intermarriage and sex crimes. While not necessarily related, these two problems are the ones which forced integration will surely magnify. These dual problems must be considered from the point of view of the history and the traditions of the South. Easterners and northerners and, for that matter, far-westerners may regard these problems in a different light, but that is their prerogative. The South claims the same prerogative for itself. If one travels throughout the South, he will run into the statement, oft repeated, that the southern Negro is not yet ready intellectually or morally for integration into the white schools. This is not intended as a reflection upon any person, because the vast majority of the Negro race, as the majority of the white race, deplores even the possibilities of intermarriage. They want to create no opportunity for sex crimes.

Nevertheless, those who have to live with the problems must face the fact that, if integration is suddenly forced upon the southern schools, such opportunities will be created. Among the Negro students in some of the integrated southern schools one would find large Negro boys, 15 and 16 years of age, sexually matured, who had not advanced as far in scholastic work as other children of their ages, placed in close association with the little white girls of more tender years. When this occurs, the stage is already set for tragedy that few doubt would occur somewhere soon. The ravishing and murder of one of these little white girls will set in motion hatred and violence which both races in the South would like to avoid. The South knows that it is not necessary or right to set the stage for such possibilities.

If one can believe what they say in public and in print, the imps who have been stoking the fire which we mentioned in the opening of this book would fan the flames of hate if they had a sensational interracial incident in the South to use as an example.

Through a lack of knowledge of the facts, non-southerners have created for themselves, and for the South, many needless racial problems. Apparently they have always recognized that there were many different kinds and types of white people, but they insisted on casting all Negroes in the same mold. This lack of understanding has created racial strife and bitterness in the North and East which is completely unknown in the South. These developments are reported almost daily in the press but otherwise ignored. It is not too farfetched to say that the residents of many, if not all, of the exclusively white residential neighborhoods in the North and East live in fear of the day when Negroes will acquire property and move into the neighborhood. Many of these same people advocate forcing integration upon the South, and yet they sell their homes at a great financial sacrifice and move to other exclusive locations when their own communities become "integrated."

Examples of the failure of non-southern States to deal fairly and efficiently with the racial problem could be extended to infinity. No doubt, these failures stem from a basic lack of understanding of the problem. The fact remains that there is no royal road to such understanding and that social problems and the exercise of police power are essential problems for each State and locality. They are not problems addressing themselves to the federal government; and they are not problems that can be solved by an over-all panacea.

Let it be said to the credit of the South that it has never attempted to enforce its philosophy or way of life upon the rest of the nation. It has suffered, usually in silence, the "slings and arrows" of outrageous propaganda.

PROPAGANDA ANTICS

It has been very interesting indeed to observe the verbal gymnastics of these propagandists. They magnify and distort every racial clash in the South and tend to ignore even worse episodes in States where there is segregation but no laws requiring segregation. A few years ago, an undetermined but a large number of Negroes were killed in race riots in Detroit, Michigan known as the "Bell Isle race riots." During the first World War and immediately thereafter race riots in and near Philadelphia, Pennsylvania reached such proportions that the Marines were called in to patrol the streets.

Numerous northern cities have had racial clashes far more bloody than the South has ever experienced.

In an Associated Press dispatch dated April 6, 1956, appeared the following news item from California:

> With blood spurting from a self-inflicted gash in his throat, Robert O. Pierce, 27-year-old gunman, died in the gas chamber today in "the most violent execution" in San Quentin's history, screaming, "I'm innocent! I'm innocent!"
>
> Pierce fought, cursed, and pleaded to God up to the moment of his death at 10:15 A.M.
>
> Both men were Negroes. (Two men were executed for the crime of murder and robbery.)
>
> "I'm innocent," Pierce screamed as four guards dragged him to the gas chamber, "I'm innocent. Don't let me go like this, God!"

If any of the foregoing had occurred in the South, great would have been the hue and cry of "southern prejudice," "southern cruelty," and "southern barbarism." Unfortunately, some deplorable events have occurred in the South, and the South has not been able to forget them. Is racial killing, discrimination, lynching, or legal execution right and proper in a State which has no laws against integration or miscegenation and wrong in a State that has such legal or constitutional provisions? It would seem so to the southerner. It seems to him that everything that can be done to fan the flames of prejudice against the South, to create racial strife and bitterness, and to increase the racial problem is being done. Southerners will not try to pass upon the judgment of the California courts which permitted Robert O. Pierce, protesting his innocence, to be carried to his execution.

That is a question, as far as the southerner is concerned, that addresses itself to the people and the courts of the State of California. The southerner believes that if each State is not capable of preserving law and order and in meting out justice in its own confines that certainly no other State or group of States is capable of doing so and our system of government is doomed.

The following item appeared in a United Press dispatch under dateline of April 19, 1956:

> A teen-aged "wolf pack" confessed yesterday to at least twenty-five cases of ravishing, and one member of the gang admitted the bludgeon slaying of an elderly woman, police said.
>
> The gang included three 15-year-olds and youths aged 17 and 19 who terrorized the city's near East Side for nearly six months. Homicide detectives said last night they believed more boys were involved and that the five held would be questioned further before charges were placed.
>
> A strapping, 200-pound 17-year-old admitted the slaying of 64-year-old Mrs. Eleanor Biegalski last Oct. 15 by smashing her skull with a brick, police

said. The youth, Willis Harris, Jr., who stands 6 feet 3½ inches, confessed to beating the woman in an alley and then dragging her to a yard near her home where he assaulted her as she lay unconscious.

Other members of the Negro gang admitted criminally assaulting at least twenty-five women, including a Negro nurse, detectives said.

The following official reference will help to demonstrate that the foregoing analysis can be officially confirmed. The case quoted below is just one of many.

In the case of Wilbert K. Slaton *vs.* The City of Chicago, Appellate Court of Illinois, First District, Nov. 22, 1955, 130 N.E. 2d 205, the following state of facts is detailed concerning an occurrence in the City of Chicago.

The record reveals that on the 14th day of August, 1947, there was located on the east side of Halstead Street between 103rd and 105th Streets a public housing development known as the Fernwood Park Housing Development. The project consisted of 67 apartments, eight of which were occupied by Negro families and the rest by white families. The Negro families moved into the project on August 12, 1947, two days before the incident in question. The next day more than a thousand people assembled on the streets surrounding the project and threatened to evict the Negro families. On the day in question between the hours of 9:00 and 11:00 o'clock P.M. several thousand persons had assembled about the project. The crowd was dense, and traffic on Halstead Street was impeded and blocked for over two hours from 100th to 105th Streets, including the intersection of 103rd and Halstead Streets. Its members stopped cars and opened their doors to find out if there were any Ne-

groes in them. In one instance a taxicab was
stopped and examined. Some of the crowd said,
"There aren't any niggers in there. Let 'em go. We
are going to run the niggers out of the project—get
'em out of here." A large number of policemen
were assigned to the scene. The unlawful assembly
of people was armed with bats, sticks, bricks, and
stones. On some occasions stones and bricks were
thrown.

Between 11:00 and 12:00 o'clock midnight, plaintiff was driving north on Halstead Street. He was
detoured by police officers at 107th Street to Pe-
oria Street, where his automobile was again detoured by other police north to 103rd Street. There
the detour by the police ended. Plaintiff proceeded east on 103rd Street to drive back to Halstead
Street. A large crowd had gathered at the intersection of 103rd and Halstead Streets. They started
yelling, "Niggers! Here comes a bunch of niggers!
Get that nigger driver in that car! What is that
black son-of-a-bitch doing driving through here?
Get that nigger driver of that car!" Plaintiff started
to turn northward into Halstead Street when members of the crowd started throwing bricks at the
car and its occupants. One of them struck the plaintiff on the right side of the skull and another struck
a woman occupant of the automobile. Other mis-
siles struck various parts of the automobile. Plaintiff
was rendered unconscious momentarily and was
bleeding profusely. He revived sufficiently to operate his automobile northward along Halstead
Street. When he reached 60th Street and Washington Park he stopped the car and turned its wheel
over to one of his companions, who drove it to
Provident Hospital and later to the County Hospital where plaintiff was given treatment and his
head wound stitched.

Nevertheless, when a Chicago Negro boy, apparently matured, or at least matured enough that he bragged that he had "had white women before," came down to the State of Mississippi and was either killed or disappeared, the press, radio, and television of a great portion of the nation became the tools of the propagandists and heaped a mountain of abuse upon the entire Southland. Contrary to propaganda, and possibly to popular belief, no rational person in the South—and that includes this writer—advocates or condones either mob violence or private killing in violation of the law. Yet when this young man, or boy, came to the South and in a boastful and arrogant manner laid hands upon and made an indecent proposal to the wife of a southern man, who apparently himself had little education but had fought for his country and would resent such an insult to his wife, trouble was inevitable. The Negro boy—or a body which was claimed to be his—was later found several miles away, having been brutally murdered. Failure of the Mississippi court to convict two men, one of them the husband, who were tried for this crime brought a further flood of abuse from the North and East.

Shortly after this unfortunate incident, the writer happened to be in the State of Mississippi, and the aftermath of these events in the minds of the people there bore no relation to the reports given on the radio and in the press. The people of Mississippi sincerely regretted the incident. The sentiment was apparently unanimous that under similar conditions almost any red-blooded white man in the South would protect his wife against a similar insult or assault. They did not approve of the killing, if indeed the Till boy were killed. The Mississippi citizens also unanimously deplored the action of the N.A.A.C.P. and other hate groups in using this unfortunate incident as a pretext for launching further attacks upon the way of life of the southern people.

It might be interesting to the people in other sections of the country to know that the southern Negro generally did not adopt the Till boy as an abused and martyred member of their race. True they deplored his killing, if indeed he were killed. But they expressed their opinions, as the white people generally did, that the actions of the Till boy were wrong and calculated to generate hatred, bitterness, and violence.

Life Magazine, under date of October 3, 1955, published an article claiming in effect, that Emmet Till's father, Private Louis Till, while a soldier in the Army of the United States, lost his life in Europe; giving his life for the American proposition that all men are equal. This article made it appear that Private Louis Till had made the supreme sacrifice upon the altar of liberty, as a soldier of his country. The inference was that Private Louis Till was either killed in battle, or lost his life in the performance of his military duties.

Authoritative sources, however, reveal an entirely different state of facts. It actually appears that instead of dying a hero's death, and thereby sharing the halo of the thousands who actually died in the service of their country, that Private Louis Till came to his death at the end of a hangman's rope in Italy, for the crimes of rape and murder. It further appeared that he had kidnaped three Italian women, Zanchi, Lucretzia and Mari, that he raped at least two of them and killed the other with his bare hands.

The foregoing is a very dramatic example of just how far afield the public can be led when caught in the current of a stream of propaganda.

One of the most eminent lawyers of Mississippi made some enlightening comments on the Till case. He had no professional connection with the case. This lawyer is well educated, well traveled and is married to a very fine lady who is a native of New England. He possesses none of the venom or prejudice which is usually attributed to public men in the deep South on any question involving racial problems. He said that he had kept up with the Till case and, in his judgment, there was not sufficient evidence before the jury to convict the two white defendants; and if the jury had brought a verdict of guilty, the verdict would certainly not have stood the test in the appellate courts. He made the remark that if the same men had been on trial for the same offense with the same evidence introduced in any part of the United States, the verdict would of necessity have been the same. He paid a very high compliment to the judge and the attorneys trying the lawsuit, laying special emphasis upon the judge's evident fairness and impartiality.

EVEN TO FOREIGN SHORES

An incident which shows the tremendous and often harmful effects of militant propaganda, involved a visitor which this Mississippi lawyer had from England. This English lady desired to visit him and his family, who were relatives of hers. The lady's husband was very reluctant to allow her to travel to Mississippi from a place where she was visiting in New England.

Having read in the newspapers and heard over the British Broadcasting Company of the terrible stories of barbarism, lynching, lawlessness, and racial strife in the South, he was actually afraid for her to make the trip. He even inquired if she should not arrange for bodyguards in order to insure her safe passage and arrival at her destination. One can imagine the good lady's somewhat happy and relieved embarrassment when she arrived at one of the beautiful southern cities to find herself amid happy surroundings in an atmosphere of gracious living, with absolutely no evidence of barbarism or violence, but ample evidence of peace and good will between the races.

THE AUTHERINE LUCY CASE

The much publicized case of Autherine Lucy, the 26-year-old Negro woman who tried to enter the University of Alabama, is another outstanding example of a deliberate attempt to create strife and friction for propaganda purposes. Miss Lucy, according to the press, had been a member of the N.A.A.C.P. for several years. That organization seems to have inspired, guided, and reported her every thought and action. Her parents, again according to news and press reports, implored her to give up the plan.

The manner in which she applied to the university, the outside agitators who accompanied and counseled her, and the extensive publicity given her actions demonstrated that it was no ordinary event. The people of Alabama and the South recognized—if the rest of the country did not—that here was no innocent and demure little girl, a victim of racial bigotry, being refused admittance to a State school to continue her search for knowledge. They saw instead a mature woman, for several years a member of a secret organization which has refused to disclose its membership to State authorities, permitting herself to be used as a guinea pig for an N.A.A.C.P. test case.

Negroes do attend some State universities in the South. Louisiana State University at Baton Rouge has about 20 Negro students, most or perhaps all of them in the graduate schools. The University of Tennessee also has Negro students enrolled. There were available Negro schools and white schools into which Miss Lucy would have been accepted. She and her advisors knew that, and they also knew that under the laws of Alabama and the rules of its university she would not be allowed to enter that school.

The only logical conclusion is that the entire episode was created in order to further a propaganda campaign. It was one more step in the plan and design to subvert local and State laws and to supplant them with the newly declared policy of the federal judiciary. The N.A.A.C.P. has said, and will no doubt continue to say, that it desires only to force the University of Alabama (and, of course, all of the South) to obey the federal law. Here is the weakness of that argument. *There is no federal law to that effect. There is no federal law denouncing segregation in public schools. There is no law requiring integration of the races in public schools or anywhere else.*

WHAT DO SOUTHERN NEGROES THINK
OF FORCED INTEGRATION?

All of us form our opinions from what we see, hear, and experience. Our opinions are good or bad, wise, foolish, or indifferent, depending upon whether that which we see, hear, and experience is true or false, good or bad. It is this truism which makes it imperative that no effort be spared to give a full, complete, and true picture of the racial problem in the South to the world and particularly to the rest of the United States.

At Carson Newman College, Jefferson City, Tennessee about the year of 1924 or 1925, there appeared upon the chapel platform one morning a Negro guest who was introduced as the speaker of the morning and was extended the unusual privilege of utilizing as much time as he desired. From almost the first word he held his audience enthralled. He was an eloquent and forceful speaker. He spoke for almost two hours, never using an adjective for the second time if another one would fit better. His discussion of the Negro in the South turned out to be as prophetic as it was profound.

Even at that time there was considerable agitation looking toward integration in public schools in the South and intermarriage between the races in the South. This was possibly an illegitimate offshoot of many sincere and genuine efforts that were being made by leaders of both races to: improve the educational facilities for the Negro in the South; to prepare him for, and to obtain for him, the rights as a citizen which he was guaranteed under the Constitution; and to help him achieve a more desirable place in the economy of the South so that his standard of living might be

102

improved. There was also much talk at that time of what was known as "social equality."

The following quotation may not be exact or couched in language quite as eloquent as that used by the speaker; but it does portray his approach to this problem, one that will stand the test of time.

The American Negro has achieved more in a shorter length of time than any race of people in the history of mankind. Approximately 60 years ago the shackles of slavery were stricken from his limbs. Less than 300 years ago he was in complete savagery. The strides that he has made in that short interval in education, the sciences, agriculture, in physical and mental development are unparalleled in the history of the world. He has developed leaders who have helped to lead his race out of the wilderness. These accomplishments have been possible because he has had the advantage of drawing upon the reservoir of knowledge acquired by the white race in the last 5,000 years. He has added to the advantages given to him by the white race his own natural finesse.

It would not be fair or truthful to say that the Negro in America has accomplished all that he has set out to accomplish or that could be accomplished. In many respects he has lagged behind; and in a great many respects he has not had the educational advantages which were necessary for his improvement. Some of these advantages have been withheld from him for reasons of history, traditions, prejudice, and genuine fear. Perhaps the greatest drawback to the advancement of the Negro in the South has been the impoverished condition in which this section found itself following the bloody strife of the Civil War.

We hear much of "social equality." This is a fictitious term, an empty phrase, a snare and a delusion. The Negro likes to be with his own kind. He wants the right to be with his own kind even as the white race wants the same right. But he wants an education. He wants schools, colleges, and educational facilities which will give him equal advantage with his white brethren. He wants to learn how to assume, and he wants to assume, the duties of citizenship and exercise all the functions of a citizen. He wants, and is entitled to, the right to vote as a free citizen of a free country. He does not want, and it would not be good for him to have, something given to him for nothing. He does not want, nor would it be to his advantage, to be placed by force in any position that he could not honestly fill upon his own merits. The American Negro will eventually fill that place in society, politics, business, commerce, and industry that he is qualified to fill because of his intellectual attainments and his moral fiber.

Booker T. Washington was one of the greatest, and possibly one of the best known, leaders of the Negro race of a generation ago. His philosophy is just as scholarly and convincing now as when he uttered the following quotation in a speech made by him on September 18, 1895, at the opening of the Atlanta Exhibition:

"The wisest among my race understand that the agitation of questions of social equality is the extremest folly, and that progress in the enjoyment of all the privileges that will come to us must be the result of severe and constant struggle rather than of artificial forcing. No race that has anything to contribute to the markets of the world is long in any degree ostracized. It is important and right that all privileges of the law be ours, but it is vastly more important that we be prepared for the exercise of these privileges. The opportunity to earn a dollar in a factory just now is worth infinitely more than the opportunity to spend a dollar in an opera house."

Forced integration most certainly would be included in what this renowned Negro leader described as "artificial forcing." If his philosophy could prevail, the southern Negro could live in peaceful coexistence, as he has learned to do with his white neighbor, and qualify himself to occupy, without force or special privilege, an estimable position in organized society, one which he will be able to assume with dignity and a sense of achievement.

WHAT ARE SOUTHERNERS THINKING NOW?

Mound Bayou, Mississippi is an all-Negro town, the largest such town in the United States. It was settled originally by two men named Green and Montgomery who were freed slaves of Joe Davis, brother of Jefferson Davis, President of the Confederacy. A dignified marker on the highway on the outskirts of the small town announces it as the largest all-Negro town in the United States. It is not stated just what method is used to prevent white people from moving into the town or establishing themselves there. The probable answer is that the whites respect the rights of the Negroes to have an all-Negro town if they want one. In any event, there appears not the slightest dissension about the matter.

The existence of this town, and others like it, provokes the thought that if the present trend toward forced integration continues that it will be just as unlawful for the Negroes to have all-Negro schools, all-Negro towns, or clubs, fraternities, societies, or recreational facilities exclusively for Negroes as it will be for the whites to have all-white institutions of the same kind. Or do the integrationists propose forced integration only against the whites and not against the Negroes?

The mayor of Mound Bayou is Mr. Benjamin A. Green, a son of one of the founders. He is a courteous, intelligent gentleman, a graduate of Fisk University and of Harvard Law School of the class of 1914. His long and useful life has been spent in the practice of law and in the service of his people in Mound Bayou. In him one finds the type of man to whom the Negroes look, and should continue to look, for leadership. His concern appears to be solely for the wel-

fare of his town and people. The procurement of industry
in Mound Bayou in order to give employment to, and raise
the standard of living of, the citizens of that community
seems to be his prime objective. Pressed for a statement on
the question of integration, he gave one that was both suc-
cinct and brief:

"Integration of the races in the southern schools and institutions will eventually come. When it does come, it will be
through education and tolerance and not through force.
Passing a law, or repealing a law, cannot bring it about;
neither can the decision of a court. There remains much
educational work to be done both with the Negro and the
white people in the South before integration is a possibility.
The southern Negro is not ready for integration, either intellectually or morally. Much of this is the fault of the white
man because he has not been willing, and many times has
not been able financially, to provide the Negro with the
educational opportunities which he needs to equip him for
integration and for carrying on his duties as a citizen of his
State and community."

Mr. Green's concluding statement was exceptionally significant:

"It is not the southern Negro who is stirring up this integration squabble. It is being fomented by outsiders who
know little or nothing about our problems down here and
who care less."

The following very interestng article appeared as an Associated Press dispatch, with the date line of Lakeland,
Florida, March 20, 1956:

Speaking at a meeting of white and Negro citizens honored by the Lakeland Negro Elks Club for
community service, a Negro educator told Negroes
last night that there are more important things to
concern themselves with than segregation.

"Don't worry about Autherine Lucy and Alabama," said Maxwell W. Saxon of Bethune-Cookman College at Daytona Beach. "Worry about conditions where you are. Clean up your own back yard. Don't promote any race fight."

Saxon, assistant director of the development program at Bethune-Cookman, spoke to about 300 Negroes and a scattering of white persons seated on a nonsegregated basis.

Seven white persons were among the score receiving awards from the Negro Elks Club for community service for both races.

Ed R. Bentley, white Lakeland lawyer and one of those honored, said this was "a most significant meeting of the two races." He said the two races "are building a State and a nation side by side."

Other white persons receiving awards included a lumberman and real-estate man who helped Negroes get better housing, a city nurse, a school-board member and Sheriff Pat Gordon and Police Chief Leo Brooker, both of whom have Negroes on their forces.

"Integration and desegregation are things you can't do by force," Saxon said. "Education and time are the two major factors."

He said, "I could not advocate going to school with white people."

Newspaper editors, by the very nature of their training and work, must be familiar with the situations existing in their respective cities or communities, particularly if the subject is of grave importance. The *U.S. News and World Report*, in its issue of February 24, 1956, contained a report of question-and-answer interviews with the editors of fifteen newspapers in the South. Practically without exception, these men state that racial relations in the South had worsened considerably since the Supreme Court decision

in the school cases. Their statements as to conditions in
their respective States and communities strongly support
conclusions which we have already expressed. Because their
statements are so persuasive and pertinent, we quote a few
significant excerpts from the *U.S. News and World Report*
of that date. (Used by permission.)

One of those interviewed was the editor of a Negro newspaper. He was MR. PERCY GREENE of the *JACKSON,
MISSISSIPPI ADVOCATE*. His answers to questions were
most enlightening.

> Q. Mr. Green, as editor of a Negro newspaper,
> how do you find conditions since the decision on
> desegregation by the Supreme Court?
>
> A. I think they are very much worse.
>
> Q. Worse than a year or two ago?
>
> A. The situation is infinitely worse than it was
> in 1953.
>
> Q. You feel, then, that lines between the races
> are hardening?
>
> A. Yes, definitely. Negroes have become vic-
> tims of hate and frustration and a kind of apathy;
> hate engendered by the propaganda to which they
> are being subjected from various sections of the
> Negro press and certain sections of Negro leader-
> ship, and by the opposition of the prosegregation
> groups, such as the Citizens Councils, in the South.
> And apathy from being told that there is a short
> cut—for instance, that the decision of the Supreme
> Court relieves the Negro of any personal individual
> responsibility at the local level, in co-operation with
> the white people, to try and work out these prob-
> lems.
>
> Q. That it is going to be handled from above
> and he doesn't have to do anything about it?
>
> A. That's right.
>
> Q. Is there any impression that the national

government might use troops to enforce desegregation?

A.   Well, you see, that impression has gotten
around. I think it is mainly one of the psychological
effects of the type of things that Negroes are reading and that Negro speakers are saying—that Negroes themselves are looking forward to the day
when they can see somebody come down here and
force these people to do something they don't want
to do.

*I don't think among intelligent Negroes that
there is any such hope or that it is a prospect within
the immediate future. . . .*

It's creating the frustration and fear and hate in
them. Of course, none of that is coming to pass.

Q.   What do you think is responsible for the intense feeling in the South on this question of mixed
schools?

A.   The spreading of the idea that the Negro's
No. 1 ambition is not equality under the law but association with white people. The idea has been
fostered by the fact that some Negro leaders have
divorced their Negro wives and married white
women. Southern congressmen know about these
things—they feel that is the No. 1 objective of the
Negro.

You see, I was born and raised in Mississippi, in
the South. I am 55 years old and I took a direct
leadership in advocating that the Negro have the
right to vote long before any of these other people
who are talking now had anything to do with the
N.A.A.C.P. and I had responsible white people
helping in doing that.

I say that there is nothing going to happen in
the South of any good until a program can be laid
down which will enable intelligent white people
and Negroes to get together, even if it is a compro-

mise of the decision—the implication of the decision—of the U. S. Supreme Court.

BUFORD BOONE, publisher of the *TUSCALOOSA, ALABAMA NEWS*:

Q. Mr. Boone, do you feel that progress may have been slowed down since the Supreme Court decision against segregated schools?

A. That is a hard thing to say, because I think your reference to progress is an attempt to grasp a problem which is primarily a problem of men's minds. . . .

The problems down here are terrific. I made a statement recently to the effect that it may be silly to some people to revere a cow, but it isn't to the Hindus. And it may be un-Christian, it may be un-American, and it may be unpatriotic in the minds of some for southerners to feel as they do about segregation. But it is far past a state of mind; it is something that is actual; it is something that exists. And whether it is right or wrong, it is a state that must be considered in trying to arrive at a just and fair conclusion. . . .

Q. Do southerners feel that there is perhaps some hypocrisy in the criticism by northerners.

A. Yes, they do. A great deal of it is defensive mechanism, and a great deal of it isn't. We point out that there have been worse race riots in Detroit and Chicago than there have been in any southern city. And we, as a section and as an area, take considerable comfort from the fact that there have been situations in other parts of the country, from which we feel that we are getting a great deal of criticism, that have been worse than any situations we have had in our part of the country.

GROVER C. HALL, JR., EDITOR, *MONTGOMERY, ALABAMA ADVERTISER*:

Q. In your opinion, Mr. Hall, are relations between the races in the South better than they were, or not so good as they were, before the Supreme Court decision?

A. Confining my answer to Alabama, there is not the slightest question but what they have degenerated in a saddening way. I see otherwise reasonable people who are now quite aroused about this thing.

You find, for example, that here in Montgomery where we have had the boycott of the bus system by Negroes that they have gotten what the "eggheads" call "polarized"—you've got the whites drawn up in one group and the colored in the other group.

Q. Has the progress toward good relations been slowed down since the decision on segregated schools, then?

A. It has. You've got the backs of the whites pretty well set now. They are frightened. . . .

JAMES G. STAHLMAN, PUBLISHER OF THE *NASHVILLE, TENNESSEE BANNER*:

Q. In your opinion, Mr. Stahlman, are relations between the races in the South better than before the Supreme Court decision against segregated schools or not so good?

A. Not nearly so good. I think the University of Alabama episode is a sample. All of this intense feeling has been engendered largely, I would say, as a result of resentment toward the N.A.A.C.P. I think the N.A.A.C.P. has done more to create this situation in the South than any other one agency.

I don't think there is going to be any real solution to this problem down here until all the outsiders are clear out of this picture. Then, let the southern white people of good will and the southern Negroes of good will settle this thing between them. . . .

Q.   Why is the feeling so intense in the South on this issue?

A.   I think it is a lot more deep-seated down here than the people elsewhere in the country have ever been willing to recognize. I think it is a hangover from Reconstruction days when the South was occupied. I don't think the South has gotten entirely over that. I think it was on the way out of it until this thing came along.

People down here just don't believe in a social mixing of the races. We want to give the Negro every opportunity to live as a free man in this country, as he is entitled to live under the law. We want to give him every advantage he can possibly have in the way of public conveyance, public instruction, and the rest of it, so far as he is able to absorb it. But there are a lot of us who don't want any social integration in any particular, and a lot of us are determined that it isn't going to happen so long as we can do anything about it legally.

THOMAS WARING, EDITOR, *THE CHARLESTON, SOUTH CAROLINA NEWS AND COURIER*:

Q.   In your opinion, Mr. Waring, are relations between the races in the South better or not as good as they were before the Supreme Court decision against segregated schools?

A.   They're definitely less good.

Q.   Would you say in your section that there is

any danger of violence if moves are made for immediate enforcement of the decision?

A. I believe there would be danger of difficulties. In fact, I've just gotten some reports today,
which indicate to me that there's a certain amount
of tension here in the city, where race relations in
the past have been extremely cordial and good, and
they're rather disturbing to us.

Q. Why do you think, basically, the feeling is
so intense in the South on this issue? Is the objection to mixed schools largely on social grounds?

A. Social grounds, yes; that covers a good deal
of territory. I would say that covers an awful lot of
reasons. There are many reasons, and "social
grounds" perhaps covers as many of them as you
can think of. But I believe the truth of the matter
is that there's an underlying fear of eventual amalgamation of the races, meaning miscegenation, intermarriage, or whatever you want to call it. I think
the majority of white people in the southern region
with which I am familiar do not want that to happen. . . .

Q. Do you think southerners feel that perhaps
there's some hypocrisy in the attitude of northerners, that perhaps people of the North are overlook-
ing a considerable degree of segregation in their
own parts of the country?

A. Well, certainly in some places you could call
it hypocrisy. I think in a good many instances,
probably the majority of instances, it's a lack of
understanding of what is going on.

We feel, however, that one of the main reasons
why those people in glass houses are throwing
stones is that they have been misled as to what the
true conditions are in the South. We feel that if
they understood and had been given proper information by the newspapers and magazines, they

would not be so bitter in their condemnation of the South. They would understand that the southern pattern is not a cruel or vindictive or hateful way of treating colored people but is simply a necessary way of getting along.

I believe they would understand that the colored people are far better off than they have been led to believe.

I have said and written several times that with the very notable exception of *U. S. News and World Report,* which has been very fair and complete on this subject, the national press has abandoned objectivity in its reporting of the southern and racial issues.

C. P. LITER, EXECUTIVE EDITOR, *THE BATON ROUGE, LOUISIANA ADVOCATE AND STATE TIMES:*

Q. Mr. Liter, why do you feel there's such opposition, such intense feeling in the South on the issue of mixed schools?

A. I think the old feeling is that the worlds of the blacks and the whites are not the same—sparrows don't associate with jay birds and robins. The whites feel that they're entitled to be by themselves if they want to be, and that the colored people are entitled to be by themselves.

We have a Negro section here in town where they have a theatre which is equal to any that the White people have; they have their own drugstore —I'm talking about a shopping center now—and they have their own barber-shop. This particular section is a perfect example of how the Negroes have an opportunity to be business men among their own people, where they wouldn't have the same opportunity among other people.

HODDING CARTER, EDITOR, *THE DELTA DEMO-CRAT-TIMES*, GREENVILLE, MISSISSIPPI:

Q. Mr. Carter, how long do you think it will be before separate schools are ended in Mississippi?

A. It will vary from possibly a few years, in areas of relatively small Negro concentration, to as far ahead as I can see in other areas. I really don't think there is going to be any meaningful integration in Mississippi for years.

It is impossible to figure out when, because they have so many legal devices, including the abolition of the public-school system, even before they start resorting to other kinds of pressure—economic and the like. Well, I just can't see it until ten or fifteen years, or twenty years, or longer. . . .

Q. What about relations between the races—do they appear to have changed since the decision on segregation?

A. I think they have steadily worsened since the Supreme Court decision.

Q. To the extent there's danger of violence?

A. I would say that in the areas of greatest Negro concentration and the same areas where you may have a greater cultural disparity, I believe there is a chance of violence. I don't think there is as much chance of violence in the large communities that are adequately policed as there is in the smaller ones, but most of the towns affected are small towns.

Q. Why is feeling so intense on this issue of mixed schools?

A. I think this is a delayed reaction—by and large, folks were a little stunned at first and hadn't really started thinking about a counterattack. But as for the opposition to mixed schools, I think you can't get over something that has been not only sus-

tained by the Court but is part of the folkways of
the white people down here for a hundred years.

I think we do have, too, a southern resentment of
many generations' standing of federal interference
with what is thought to be local self-government.

FREDERICK SULLENS, EDITOR, *THE JACKSON,
MISSISSIPPI NEWS*:

Q. Mr. Sullens, why do you think the feeling
is so intense in the South on the segregation issue?
What is the basic, underlying objection to mixed
schools?

A. The basic, underlying objection is that it is
opposed to the southern way of life, the traditions
and customs that are very precious to our people.
We feel that integration is merely the first step, or
an opening wedge, toward mixed marriages, miscegenation, and the mongrelization of the human
race.

Q. How long, in your opinion, will it be before
separate schools are ended in Mississippi?

A. I don't think that mixed schools will ever
come to pass in Mississippi.

Q. Do you think there's a possibility of danger
of violence if moves are made toward immediate
enforcement of the Supreme Court decision against
segregated schools?

A. Violence will inevitably follow any hasty
movement to force Negroes into the white schools
in Mississippi.

Q. In your opinion, are relations between the
races in the South better than, or not as good as,
before the Supreme Court decision?

A. Racial relations have been strained by the
decision, of course, but not between a very large

majority of the white people and the peaceful, law-abiding, clear-thinking colored people.

Q. Do you think that progress had been made toward equal opportunities for both races prior to the decision?

A. Very satisfactory progress was being made here in Mississippi, especially in bringing about an equal but separate school system for the Negroes only a short time prior to the decision. We appropriated more than twenty million dollars for the purpose of bringing Negro schools up to a higher standard.

Q. Do you think that progress has been slowed?

A. Very much so, except that here in Mississippi, we are continuing to appropriate money in behalf of the objective we have started.

F. B. BRASWELL, EDITOR, *THE ATHENS, GEORGIA BANNER-HERALD*:

Q. Why is the feeling so intense in the South on the issue?

A. Well, my answer to that question is that for generations we have just followed a certain social pattern that we've become accustomed to. We also feel that, under this pattern, the Negro race has been given justice—in the courts and out of the courts—I think, uniformly fair treatment. Of course, there are isolated cases where that might not be true, but I'm speaking generally. That's one thing.

Another thing is that in many communities there is such a large colored population that we in the South do not feel that that element could be absorbed into the white schools conveniently and without friction of various kinds. And added to that is that great headway—almost miraculous

headway—has been made in providing them with
equal educational opportunities.

We have published articles by a colored preacher
appealing mostly to Negroes. This minister feels—
and I feel the same way—that putting these poorly
clothed colored children in school with well-dressed
white children puts the Negro children at a complete disadvantage, just from the standpoint of appearance.

After all, it is an internal matter, and Washington should be capable of regulating its own internal
affairs, just as we feel we are capable of regulating
ours.

From everywhere in the South come the same answers.
Of course there may be an isolated difference of opinion,
but, in general, they agree upon the main factors insisted
upon in these discussions. Recently, there appeared in the
KNOXVILLE JOURNAL, KNOXVILLE, TENNESSEE, a
column by EDWARD F. HUTTON, and we think it is worth
repeating:

Judge Harold Medina took a complete course in
communistic tactics. He is one of many who think
the Reds are pouring gasoline on the kindling with
reference to the school problem in the South.

Governor Harriman wants it settled at once and
mentions the use of federal troops. But did he send
the State troopers to Farmingdale, Long Island to
put down rioting mobs in the Republic Aviation's
strike, which really was a strike against national defense?

It is easy to be brave about distant matters.

Because the Supreme Court overrode its own decision of long standing on "separate but equal"
schools, various politicians beat their noble bosoms
about "nullification."

How many of them did not nullify the Volstead Act, also held constitutional by the High Court?

Vice-President Nixon gets into the act by claiming that the GOP should be given credit for the Court's school decision.

There are two dangerous situations—the southern school matter and the Israelis versus the Arabs.

Any person who tries to inflame the mob spirit in either of these matters should be a marked man from now on.

The times call for patient and moderate men.

Agree, Neighbor?

The experiences of many a traveling southerner have paralleled very closely that of a retired southern lawyer whose travels put him in close association with students and teachers in some of our great northern universities. He writes:

It seems that life here for a southerner is just one argument after another. Recently, the Till case was going full blast, and every time things quiet down there is another incident to take its place. Now it is the recent riot at the University of Alabama. I feel like a missionary surrounded by hostile natives.

The main trouble with these people is their total ignorance of conditions in the South. It is amazing to learn what distorted conception of southern life they have. In fact, the main way I am able to make any progress in argument with them is to point out this ignorance. They are used to taking the floor and preaching sanctimoniously from their mental vacuums, and it is unsettling indeed for them to be told that they are ignorant—the worst indictment a person can receive in their own minds (that is, after the charge of bigotry).

The arguments usually resolve into two main

phases: In the first phase there is a general accusation that there is no justice, no progress, and no conscience in the South, and that it is up to the North to supply these. The Negro is still a chattel à la Stepin Fechit who would immediately rise to the civilizational level of the whites were all vestiges of the evil of evils, segregation, removed. When I tell them of the very real progress that has been made at home, without their help or pressure, and made in spite of tremendous economic difficulties, and when I tell them of the general social level and mode of living among the Negroes at home, they don't know whether to call me a liar or to change their own positions.

Not wanting to call me a liar (and suspecting that I may be telling the truth), and also not wanting to change their positions, they go off on the second phase of the argument—"principle." Here they really get abstract. It is amazing how they have seized upon the "psychological trauma" argument of the Supreme Court as a justification for creating near chaos in the South. They also spout such phrases as, "Don't you believe in the federal system of government?" and, "Either you believe in equality or you don't." As for the psychological trauma, I recently read in *Commentary* about how large numbers of colored high-school graduates in the North go South where they can escape the social segregation of the North by attending legally segregated colored colleges in the South, and where they can join fraternities and sororities and have a normal social life. It would seem that the psychological trauma of the northern system is worse than that in the South. As for the "basic principles" from which they deduce their conclusions, that is where we get into a lot more debate.

On the principle argument, I am put in the uncomfortable position of having to explain beliefs I don't personally adhere to. The most startling argument to them, and one that takes a lot of the punch out of them, is to tell them that the traditional southerner *considers integration to be basically more immoral than defying the edict of the Supreme Court—that is, integration under circumstances which will tend to produce intermarriage.* These people seem never before to have considered that, to most white southerners, miscegenation is just as immoral as incest; and they consider a Supreme Court decision which paves the way to miscegenation (and this is certainly the next step the Supreme Court will take) to be as illegal as any decision could be. These people are making a god out of the Supreme Court.

My personal dilemma is that I believe that segregation is necessary in many parts of the South today, but I don't believe in it as a moral principle. I have resolved this dilemma by realizing that democracy is only possible through compromise, compromise by majorities by not ramming their opinions arbitrarily down the throats of minorities, and compromise with ideals by acknowledging that you can't put all your ideals into practice to their fullest extent.

In the *KNOXVILLE NEWS SENTINEL* (TENNESSEE) of very recent date, there appeared an article by the columnist Mrs. Walter Ferguson, entitled *"The South Asked for It"*:

Our present dilemma about school segregation shows how easy it is for men to throw away their freedom.

Only a few years ago, many Democrats and Republicans were delighted to give up States rights and gleefully handed over local powers to the federal government. The few voices that warned of dangers ahead were laughed into silence. Expediency of the moment was what mattered.

During the Roosevelt and Truman regimes, the predominating feeling in the Deep South, and in many other sections, was that Washington should have more authority. Millions of Americans, without any thought of tomorrow, whooped it up for federal controls. Any small cash handout from Uncle Sam brought them swiftly to heel. Little by little, local governments relinquished their rights to govern themselves in favor of federal controls.

Now we face the results of this careless attitude toward the protection of our basic liberties. And all honest men and women must admit that the segregation issue is a problem that will take statesmanship of the highest order to solve—with a lot of Christian tolerance thrown in for good measure.

I do not know which side of the question you may be on. I wish only to point out that we now see what happens to people and commonwealths who are careless of their rights to govern themselves.

When States deliberately give their liberties away, it isn't easy to get them back.

MR. ANDREW TULLY, SCRIPPS-HOWARD STAFF WRITER, on a recent journey to the South, wrote a series of articles, some of which are most interesting. As one reads Mr. Tully's articles, he gets the impression that here is a man who entered upon his tasks with a tremendous amount of prejudice but was gradually getting his eyes open. The following excerpt from an article by him will illustrate what we mean:

Hattiesburg, Mississippi, April 2—In Tunica County of Northwestern Mississippi—heart of the cotton-planting country—H. B. Cargile, planter and segregationist, surveyed as much as his eye could take in of his 1,700 acres and sighed.

"It's our fault," he said, running a hand through his unruly gray hair. "We haven't prepared them."

"Them" is what is known in Mississippi as the "cotton-patch nigger." This is the Negro who works the cotton fields as a sharecropper or as a "runner" who supplies his own equipment and seed, sharing in the profits of the soil.

Cargile's admission, in a sense, is a victory for the integration he spurns. Today, as a result of the Supreme Court decision banning school segregation, planters have to start thinking about them.

It is for them a depressing thought. Cargile would not discuss the Negro's status except to say that, "He won't be ready for responsible citizenship for at least twenty years."

But driving down and across Mississippi, through Greenville and Yazoo City, you hear the same appraisal—one that brands the field Negro as immoral, unclean, and lawless.

The stories are dreadfully identical—and they are told as a valid argument for the whites' refusal to accept the Negro in the schools or at any level.

A cook here with seven children by seven different men. A cotton-chopper there living in incest with his own children. Total absence of hygiene in the two- and three-room wooden shacks, without plumbing, that are home to the field Negroes.

Even a northerner, seeing conditions, recognizes this as one of the awful facts of life in the South.

Whatever your sympathies, it is a little easier down here to understand the militant whites' point of view.

The way it works out, for instance, there are two sets of laws—one for the whites, one for the blacks.

A white man convicted of manslaughter will be sentenced to twenty years in prison; a Negro will get off with two (if his victims are black) and then, chances are, his "boss-man" will get him out after several months because the Negro is pining away in jail and he's needed as a hand.

As for minor crimes, it is necessary to the South's economy to ignore them among Negroes. As one planter put it, "If we put every bigamous Negro in jail, we wouldn't have enough help to work our crops."

"We've got to do it," says Cargile. "We realize that now. It's the only way we can raise the Negro's standard of living—if the kids learn hygiene and morality at school, they'll take it home to their parents."

That, however, is as far as the Cargiles in Mississippi want to go. Ask them what happens when the Negro's standard of living and morality are raised to a level satisfactory to the whites, and Cargile will speak grimly for them all.

"Then," he says, "they'll still have to ram integration down my throat."

WHAT DOES COMMUNISM WANT?

Communism does not like local government. Communism requires a strong super-state or dictatorship. Communism is violently opposed to written constitutions adopted by the people after full debate. Communism prefers the autocratic authority of the party line as laid down by the dictator or clique in power at the moment. This party line can be changed from day to day, according to the whims of the dictator and the needs of the moment. Communism wants blind obedience from unquestioning followers. Traditions, legends, and even the uncontroverted facts of history are being constantly altered and tailored by the Communists to enrich their propaganda or to justify barbaric events that would not be tolerated in a democracy.

Communism refuses to be bound by legal and historic precedents. The decisions of their courts are not founded upon any constitutional or statutory law. Neither are they bottomed upon established legal principles and precedents. Instead, they proceed entirely according to the dictates of the party. For some reason, still not entirely clear, the Russians have recently admitted that many of the purge trials conducted by "people's courts" under Stalin's direction amounted to nothing more than the mass murder of political opponents. These so-called "trials," followed by execution or exile to a living death, were carried on without regard to the laws of evidence or humanity. These so-called "courts" constitute one of the chief weapons of communism. It is, therefore, easy to understand why communism would indeed be pleased with the opinion of any court which abandoned the safeguards of historic legal principles and accepted instead as its authority the writings of Communists or fellow-travelers.

Much earlier in this book reference was made to the *Daily Worker,* which is the official organ of the Communist party in this country, and how gratified that organ must be at the prospect of the bitter civil strife which the Communists undoubtedly hope and believe will follow upon any attempt to bring about, by force, integration in southern schools. The Comintern has for many years sent its disciples all over the world to spend their lives, if necessary, in any activity or endeavor which they believe would result in riots, civil strife, strikes, boycotts, and a division of the people of many nations into two or more warring factions. Thus is cultivated the ground in which the seeds of international communism are sowed. The history of the last three decades contains many classic examples of the success of this technique, which was referred to in the second World War as "fifth-column" activity.

We do not go to the extreme of suggesting that the N.A.A.C.P. is connected with the *Daily Worker* or the Communist party, although many people in the South seriously believe that it is. Neither do we mean to infer that the people of other sections of the country, and particularly the well-intentioned but misguided neighbors who are already victims of propaganda, are in any way sympatheic with the communist cause. It must be said, however, and emphasized, that many of these people, by their attitudes upon the subject based on no information except that furnished by these pressure groups, have by their adherence to the cause of integration lent much aid and comfort to such enemies of our form of government as the Communist party and the *Daily Worker.* A southern editor recently printed the following apt comment upon an article in this communist organ:

THE COMMUNISTS DO NOT LIKE THE SOUTH!

The following paragraph is from an editorial in the January 26th issue of the *Daily Worker,* the voice of communism in this country:

"The real roadblock to legislation advancing the interests of working men in general and Negroes in particular is represented by the congressional alliance of the GOP-reactionaries and the Dixiecrats. It will require the united efforts of the combined groups pledged to support civil rights to overcome this roadblock. There can be no victory against reaction if one or another part of the pro-civil-rights alliance breaks ranks and concedes defeat every time the Dixiecrat hyena howls."

The southern newspaper commented:

The South should be proud of its enemies. If any proof were needed, this one statement would confirm what is generally known to all thoughtful people in this country—that it has been the alliance of conservatives in the South with those of like mind in other parts of the nation that has saved us from communism, or to say the least, socialism, which is only a halfway step to communism. Those few southern congressmen who have refused to have a part in this alliance must realize the company they keep!

The statements made on the preceding pages, and those that will be made later, do not represent the abstract thinking of one individual. Instead they represent the composite thinking of many persons, both living and dead, from many walks of life. A studious effort has been made to give proper credit in every possible instance. If the language at times seems harsh, it is because the truth is often harsh. The outstanding individuals, statesmen, private citizens, and jurists whose opinions have been copied at some length have all faced stark reality.

From this cross-section of human experience emerge some significant facts. Briefly, they are:

1. Racial relations in the South have grown, and are growing, steadily worse since the decision of the Supreme Court of the United States in the integration cases.

2. The people of the South believe that segregation of races in educational institutions is legal, normal, and desirable; conversely, they believe forced integration of the races is legally and morally wrong and socially undesirable.

3. They believe that the majority of the whites and Negroes in the South do not desire the "full integration" envisioned by the N.A.A.C.P. nor the school integration which would be imposed by the Supreme Court decision.

4. Southern people are firmly convinced that forced integration in the South would be most harmful to the southern Negro.

5. The people of the South and the governments of the southern States believe that the Supreme Court's opinion is wrong, morally and legally; that it is based upon false beliefs and is in direct violation of the Tenth Amendment to the Constitution of the United States.

6. The southern States are *deadly serious in their intention to resist,* with all honorable means, what they consider as an unjust and illegal encroachment by the federal judiciary upon the sovereignty of the States.

7. That in the South, the white and Negro races have learned to live side by side in peaceful co-existence; and that through this arrangement, the Negro race has made great forward strides. They want this happy relationship and this progress to continue.

8. They feel that the present difficulties come not from within but without the South. They resent this outside interference because they believe it smacks of hypocrisy and springs from a lack of information and understanding.

9. In the final analysis, the solution to racial problems must rest in the hands of those who face the problem. Any solution that will preserve our form of government and stand the test of time must be arrived at through education, tolerance and mutual effort over a long period of time.

10. The southerner derives some faint hope from the fact that other decisions of the Supreme Court of the United States are meeting with equal disfavor in other sections of the nation. This hope is founded in the belief that, when the people are thoroughly aroused, they will take appropriate action to correct any mistakes that have been made. In the final analysis, that is democracy at work.

PART II

THE LAW OF THE CASE

THE LEGAL PRINCIPLES INVOLVED

Many who believe that the decision of the Supreme Court is morally wrong and fraught with the gravest dangers have been led into a despondent do-nothing attitude in the erroneous belief that, the "Supreme Court of the United States having spoken," there is nothing further that can be said or done. Such an attitude is exactly the result that the proponents of enforced integration desire. The opinion of the Supreme Court is not only morally and constitutionally wrong but, if carried out, will do great violence to the southern Negro whom it is supposed to assist and to the southern white people whom it is no doubt intended to punish. The decision itself, as a legal proposition, is unsound, erroneous, and represents a complete departure from all recognized rules of legal precedent. Many of its infirmities are apparent to a casual reader. Without entering into a highly tech-

131

nical discussion of the opinion, let us consider it in terms that the average citizen can understand.

Except in rare instances, the Supreme Court of the United States has appellate jurisdiction only. That means it can only hear cases brought to it on appeal from a lower federal court or, in some instances, from a State court. *It has no authority to declare public policy.* It can decide a case brought properly before it and, in making its decision, it can construe the statutes involved and the constitutional provisions invoked. Its decision is binding upon the litigants and establishes a precedent which other federal courts are expected to follow in similar cases. The decision of the Supreme Court, therefore, remains the interpretation of the law until it is changed either by the enactment of a statute, the amending of the Constitution, or until the Supreme Court which made the decision, or some subsequent Supreme Court, reverses it.

The proponents of integration have erroneously contended—and many of the people have accepted this contention as true—that the Supreme Court had the authority to do so and "had ordered" all southern schools of all grades to be integrated immediately. It is a sound and well-accepted proposition of law that the Supreme Court had no such authority; and that if it intended to use or attempt to use such authority, it was clearly exceeding its prerogatives.

The integration case, or cases, are Brown, *et al.*, *vs.* Board of Education of Topeka, Shawnee County, Kansas, *et al.*; Briggs, *et al.*, *vs.* Elliott, *et al.*; Davis *et al.*, *vs.* County School Board of Prince Edward County, Virginia, *et al.*; Gebhart, *et al.*, *vs.* Belton, *et al.*—and were all tried or all decided together in the Supreme Court and are reported in 347 U.S. 483, 74 *Supreme Court Reporter* 686. The opinion is short, and since so few people have had the opportunity to read it, we copy herewith the important and larger portion of the opinion. The portions which we have omitted are largely references to other cases and do not in any way effect the general tenor of the opinion.

OPINION IN SCHOOL INTEGRATION CASES

These cases come to us from the States of Kansas, South Carolina, Virginia and Delaware. They are premised on different facts and different local conditions, but a common legal question justifies their consideration together in this consolidated opinion.

In each of the cases, minors of the Negro race, through their legal representatives, seek the aid of the courts in obtaining admission to the public schools of their community on a nonsegregated basis. In each instance, they have been denied admission to schools attended by white children under laws requiring or permitting segregation according to race. This segregation was alleged to deprive the plaintiffs of the equal protection of the laws under the Fourteenth Amendment. In each of the cases other than the Delaware case, a three-judge federal district court denied relief to the plaintiffs on the so-called "separate but equal" doctrine announced by this Court in Plessy vs. Ferguson, 163 U.S. 537, 16 S. Ct. 1138, 41 L. Ed. 256. Under that doctrine, equality of treatment is accorded when the races are provided substantially equal facilities, even though these facilities be separate. In the Delaware case, the Supreme Court of Delaware adhered to that doctrine, but ordered that the plaintiffs be admitted to the white schools because of their superiority to the Negro schools.

The plaintiffs contend that segregated public schools are not "equal" and cannot be made "equal," and that hence they are deprived of the equal protection of the laws. Because of the obvious importance of the question presented, the Court took jurisdiction. Argument was heard in the 1952 term, and reargument was heard this

term on certain questions propounded by the
Court.

Reargument was largely devoted to the circumstances surrounding the adoption of the Fourteenth
Amendment in 1868. It covered exhaustively consideration of the amendment in Congress, ratification by the States, then existing practices in racial
segregation, and the views of proponents and opponents of the amendment. This discussion and our
own investigation convince us that, although these
sources cast some light, it is not enough to resolve
the problem with which we are faced. At best, they
are inconclusive. The most avid proponents of the
post-war amendments undoubtedly intended them
to remove all legal distinctions among "all persons
born or naturalized in the United States." Their
opponents, just as certainly, were antagonistic to
both the letter and the spirit of the amendments
and wished them to have the most limited effect.
What others in Congress and the State legislatures had in mind cannot be determined with any
degree of certainty.

An additional reason for the inconclusive nature
of the amendment's history, with respect to segregated schools, is the status of public education at
that time. In the South, the movement toward free
common schools, supported by general taxation,
had not yet taken hold. Education of white children was largely in the hands of private groups.
Education of Negroes was almost nonexistent, and
practically all of the race were illiterate. In fact,
any education of Negroes was forbidden by law in
some States. Today, in contrast, many Negroes
have achieved outstanding success in the arts and
sciences as well as in the business and professional
world. It is true that public-school education at the
time of the amendment had advanced further in

the North, but the effect of the amendment on northern States was generally ignored in the congressional debates. Even in the North, the conditions of public education did not approximate those existing today. The curriculum was usually rudimentary; ungraded schools were common in rural areas; the school term was but three months a year in many States; and compulsory school attendance was virtually unknown. As a consequence, it is not surprising that there should be so little in the history of the Fourteenth Amendment relating to its intended effect on public education.

In the first cases in this Court construing the Fourteenth Amendment, decided shortly after its adoption, the Court interpreted it as proscribing all State-imposed discriminations against the Negro race. The doctrine of "separate but equal" did not make its appearance in this Court until 1896, in the case of Plessy *vs.* Ferguson, *supra,* involving not education but transportation. American courts have since labored with the doctrine for over half a century. . . . And in Sweatt *vs.* Painter, *supra,* the Court expressly reserved decision on the question whether Plessy *vs.* Ferguson should be held inapplicable to public education.

In the instant cases, that question is directly presented. Here, unlike Sweatt *vs.* Painter, there are findings below that the Negro and white schools involved have been equalized, or are being equalized, with respect to buildings, curricula, qualifications, and salaries of teachers, and other "tangible" factors. Our decision, therefore, cannot turn on merely a comparison of these tangible factors in the Negro and white schools involved in each of the cases. We must look instead to the effect of segregation itself on public education.

1. In approaching this problem, we cannot turn

the clock back to 1868 when the amendment was adopted, or even to 1896 when Plessy *vs.* Ferguson was written. We must consider public education in the light of its full development and its present place in American life throughout the nation. Only in this way can it be determined if segregation in public schools deprives these plaintiffs of the equal protection of the laws.

2. Today, education is perhaps the most important function of State and local governments. Compulsory school-attendance laws and the great expenditures for education both demonstrate our recognition of the importance of education to our democratic society. It is required in the performance of our most basic public responsibilities, even service in the armed forces. It is the very foundation of good citizenship. Today, it is a principal instrument in awakening the child to cultural values, in preparing him for later professional training, and in helping him to adjust normally to his environment. In these days, it is doubtful that any child may reasonably be expected to succeed in life if he is denied the opportunity of an education. Such an opportunity, where the State has undertaken to provide it, is a right which must be made available to all on equal terms.

3. We come then to the question presented: Does segregation of children in public schools solely on the basis of race, even though the physical facilities and other "tangible" factors may be equal, deprive the children of the minority group of equal educational opportunities? We believe that it does.

In Sweatt *vs.* Painter, *supra* (339 U.S. 629, 70 S. Ct. 850), in finding that a segregated law school for Negroes could not provide them equal educational opportunities, this Court relied in large part on "those qualities which are incapable of objective measurement but which make for greatness in a law school." In McLaurin *vs.* Oklahoma State Regents, *supra* (339 U.S. 637, 70 S. Ct. 853), the Court, in requiring that a Negro admitted to a white graduate school be treated like all other students, again resorted to intangible considerations: ". . . his ability to study, to engage in discussions and exchange views with other students, and, in general, to learn his profession." Such considerations apply with added force to children in grade and high schools. To separate them from others of similar age and qualifications solely because of their race generates a feeling of inferiority as to their status in the community that may affect their hearts and minds in a way unlikely ever to be undone. The effect of this separation on their educational opportunities was well stated by a finding in the Kansas case by a court which nevertheless felt compelled to rule against the Negro plaintiffs:

"Segregation of white and colored children in public schools has a detrimental effect upon the colored children. The impact is greater when it has the sanction of the law; for the policy of separating the races is usually interpreted as denoting the inferiority of the Negro group. A sense of inferiority affects the motivation of a child to learn. Segregation with the sanction of law, therefore, has a tendency to [retard] the educational and mental development of Negro children and to deprive them of some of the benefits they would receive in a racial[ly] integrated school system."

Whatever may have been the extent of psychological knowledge at the time of Plessy *vs.* Ferguson, this finding is amply supported by modern authority. And language in Plessy *vs.* Ferguson contray to this finding is rejected.

4.   We conclude that in the field of public edu-

cation the doctrine of "separate but equal" has no
place. Separate educational facilities are inherently
unequal. Therefore, we hold that the plaintiffs and
others similarly situated for whom the actions have
been brought are, by reason of the segregation
complained of, deprived of the equal protection
of the laws guaranteed by the Fourteenth Amendment. This disposition makes unnecessary any discussion whether such segregation also violates the
Due Process Clause of the Fourteenth Amendment. . . .

*So opined the Supreme Court of the United States in a
decision destined to shake the very foundations of our
system of government.*

The prevailing and universal custom of courts in writing
opinions is to document or substantiate the opinions with
reference to other decisions of courts of equal or superior
jurisdiction and by references to State and federal statutes
and constitutional provisions. The references given by the
Supreme Court in the foregoing opinion are, for the most
part, included in footnotes which we have not copied but
which are somewhat lengthy. These footnotes refer to a
large number of federal cases, as well as State cases; but
a careful study of these cases which are cited as authority
shows that, instead of supporting the present decision of
the Supreme Court, for the most part they are in direct conflict with it and in support of the case of Plessy *vs.* Ferguson,
163 U.S. 537.

Many of the cases cited by the Supreme Court in support of its decision, or at least in the footnotes appended
to it, followed and affirmed the case of Plessy *vs.* Ferguson.
That case stood like an immovable rock in the path of political expediency. The yammer and clammer of the integrationists could not pierce the well-reasoned and expertly
written provisions of the decision in the Plessy *vs.* Ferguson
case, which has been the declared interpretation of the

constitutional provisions involved here since its publication on May 18, 1896. In order to decide the Brown case in the manner in which it was decided, it became necessary to dispose of Plessy *vs.* Ferguson, which the Supreme Court did by striking it down. Of course, in striking down the case of Plessy *vs.* Ferguson, or to put it as the Court put it, "rejecting it," the Court had also to reject the great mass of cases which had been decided by the Supreme Court of the United States and other courts under the authority of, and following the interpretation laid down in, the case of Plessy *vs.* Ferguson.

It should be borne in mind that, since the case of Plessy *vs.* Ferguson was decided, there has been no amendment to any constitution, federal or State, and no statute, federal or State, which would have the effect of repealing, modifying, or changing in the slightest the Court's interpretation of the Constitution in Plessy *vs.* Ferguson. In the final analysis the present situation reflects only the decision of, and opinion of, the present members of the Supreme Court who have thrown overboard and rejected the leading cases upon this subject for almost a hundred years.

All the cases thus "rejected" were bottomed upon the fundamentally sound basis that the federal government and, of course, the federal courts cannot assume authority. That authority must be given, if at all, by the Constitution. Otherwise it is reserved to the State or local government. Mr. Justice Brandeis, in Erie R. Co. *vs.* Tompkins, 304 U.S. 64, 58 S. Ct. 822 (decided April 25, 1938), expressed this great truth in unforgettable fashion when he said:

"As stated by Mr. Justice Field when protesting in Baltimore & Ohio R. R. Co. *vs.* Baugh, 149 U.S. 368, 401, 13 S. Ct. 914, 927, 37 L. Ed. 772, against ignoring the Ohio common law of fellow-servant liability, I am aware that what has been termed the general law of the country—which is often little less than what the judge advancing the doctrine thinks at the time should be the general law on a particular subject—has been often advanced in judicial opinions of this

Court to control a conflicting law of a State. I admit that learned judges have fallen into the habit of repeating this doctrine as a convenient mode of brushing aside the law of a State in conflict with their views. And I confess that, moved and governed by the authority of the great names of those judges, I have, myself, in many instances, unhesitatingly and confidently, but I think now erroneously, repeated the same doctrine. But notwithstanding the great names which may be cited in favor of the doctrine, and notwithstanding the frequency with which the doctrine has been reiterated, there stands, as a perpetual protest against its repetition, the Constitution of the United States, which recognizes and preserves the autonomy and independence of the States—independence in their legislative and independence in their judicial departments. Supervision over either the legislative or the judicial action of the States is in no case permissible except as to matters by the Constitution specifically authorized or delegated to the United States. Any interference with either, except as thus permitted, is an invasion of the authority of the State and, to that extent, a denial of its independence."

The foregoing is and must remain the principal issue in the Brown case. It must also be the first issue in considering the trend of the Supreme Court's recent rulings which ignore the admonition of Mr. Justice Brandeis. No amount of "social reform" or "psychological" consideration, which at best may have transient and doubtful value, can justify the abandonment of the Constitution of the United States, with its checks and balances, its guarantees of freedom, and its restraint of governmental authority.

The case of Plessy vs. Ferguson arose in the State of Louisiana and involved separate facilities for the white and Negro races in passenger railroad accommodations. The effect of that well-reasoned opinion was, and has long been interpreted to be, that the States could not deny any person equal protection of the law, but that the "equal protection" clause of the Fourteenth Amendment did not require that all races have the same facilities but substantially equal facilities. This interpretation of the Fourteenth Amendment is consistent with the terms and provisions of the Tenth Amendment, which says that all powers not delegated to the federal government nor prohibited to the States are reserved to the States and to the people. In other words the method of making available the equal facilities to the different races is held to be a matter to be decided by each State, having consideration for local conditions and the other factors prevailing. In order that we may have a better idea of what the Supreme Court in its recent decision actually overruled and "rejected" we quote here at some length from the decision in the Plessy *vs.* Ferguson case:

This case turns upon the constitutionality of an act of the General Assembly of the State of Louisiana, passed in 1890, providing for separate railway carriages for the white and colored races (Act. 1890, No. 111, p. 152).

The constitutionality of this act is attacked upon the ground that it conflicts both with the Thirteenth Amendment of the Constitution, abolishing slavery, and the Fourteenth Amendment, which prohibits certain restrictive legislation on the part of the States.

A statute which implies merely a legal distinction between the white and colored races—a distinction which is founded in the color of the two races, and which must always exist so long as white men are distinguished from the other race by color —has no tendency to destroy the legal equality of the two races or re-establish a state of involuntary servitude.

By the Fourteenth Amendment, all persons born or naturalized in the United States, and subject to the jurisdiction thereof, are made citizens of the United States and of the State wherein they reside;

and the States are forbidden from making or enforcing any law which shall abridge the privileges
or immunities of citizens of the United States, or
shall deprive any person of life, liberty, or property
without due process of law, or deny to any person
within their jurisdiction the equal protection of the
laws.

The object of the amendment was undoubtedly
to enforce the absolute equality of the two races
before the law, but in the nature of things it could
not have been intended to abolish distinctions
based upon color, or to enforce social, as distinguished from political, equality, or a commingling
of the two races upon terms unsatisfactory to either.
Laws permitting and even requiring, their separation in places where they are liable to be brought
into contact do not necessarily imply the inferiority
of either race to the other, and have been generally,
if not universally, recognized as within the compe-
tency of the State legislatures in the exercise of
their police power. The most common instance of
this is connected with the establishment of separate schools for white and colored children, which
has been held to be a valid exercise of the legislative power even by courts of States where the political rights of the colored race have been longest
and most earnestly enforced.

Laws forbidding the intermarriage of the two
races may be said in a technical sense to interfere
with the freedom of contract, and yet have been
universally recognized as within the police power
of the State (State vs. Gibson, 36 Indiana, 389).

The distinction between laws interfering with
the political equality of the Negro and those requiring the separation of the two races in schools,
theatres, and railway carriages has been frequently
drawn by this court. Thus, in Strauder vs. West

Virginia, 100 U.S. 303, it was held that a law of
West Virginia limiting to white male persons, 21
years of age and citizens of the State, the right to
sit upon juries was a discrimination which implied
a legal inferiority in civil society, which lessened
the security of the right of the colored race, and
was a step toward reducing them to a condition of
servility. Indeed, the right of a colored man that,
in the selection of jurors to pass upon his life, liberty, and property there shall be exclusion of his
race, and no discrimination against them because of
color, has been asserted in a number of cases (Vir-
giania *vs.* Rives, 100 U.S. 313; Neal *vs.* Delaware,
103 U.S. 370; Bush *vs.* Kentucky, 107 U.S. 110;
Gibson *vs.* Mississippi, 162 U.S. 565).

Much nearer, and, indeed, almost directly in
point, is the case of the Louisville, New Orleans
&c. Railway *vs.* Mississippi, 133 U.S. 587, wherein
the railway company was indicted for a violation
of a statute of Mississippi, enacting that all railroads carrying passengers should provide equal but
separate accommodations for the white and colored
races, by providing two or more passenger cars for
each passenger train, or by dividing the passenger
cars by a partition, so as to secure separate accommodations. The case was presented in a different
aspect from the one under consideration, inasmuch
as it was an indictment against the railway company for failing to provide the separate accommodations, but the question considered was the constitutionality of the law. In that case, the Supreme
Court of Mississippi, 66 Mississippi, 662, had held
that the statute applied solely to commerce within
the State, and, that being the construction of the
State statute by its highest court, was accepted as
conclusive. "If it be a matter," said the court, p.
591, "respecting commerce wholly within a State,

and not interfering with commerce between the States, then, obviously there is no violation of the commerce clause of the federal Constitution. . . ."

In the present case no question of interference with interstate commerce can possibly arise, since the East Louisiana Railway appears to have been purely a local line, with both its termini within the State of Louisiana. Similar statutes for the separation of the two races upon public conveyances were held to be constitutional in Westchester &c Railroad *vs.* Miles, 55 Penn. St. 209; Day *vs.* Owen, 5 Michigan, 520; Chicago &c. Railway *vs.* Williams, 55 Illinois, 185; Chesapeake &c. Railroad *vs.* Wells, 85 Tennessee, 613; Memphis &c. Railroad *vs.* Benson, 85 Tennessee, 627; The Sue, 22 Fed. Rep. 843; Logwood *vs.* Memphis &c. Railroad, 23 Fed. Rep. 318; McGuinn *vs.* Forbes, 37 Fed. Rep. 639; People *vs.* King, 18 N. E. Rep. 245; Houck *vs.* South Pac. Railway, 38 Fed. Rep. 226; Heard *vs.* Georgia Railroad Co., 3 Int. Com. Com'n. 111; S.C., 1, *Ibid.* 428.

While we think the enforced separation of the races, as applied to the internal commerce of the State, neither abridges the privileges or immunities of the colored man, deprives him of his property without due process of law, nor denies him the equal protection of the law, within the meaning of the Fourteenth Amendment. . . .

We consider the underlying fallacy of the plaintiff's argument to consist in the assumption that the enforced separation of the two races stamps the colored race with a badge of inferiority. If this be so, it is not by reason of anything found in the act, but solely because the colored race chooses to put that construction upon it. The argument necessarily assumes that if, as has been more than once the case, and is not unlikely to be so again, the colored race should become the dominant power in the State legislature, and should enact a law in precisely similar terms, it would thereby relegate the white race to an inferior position. We imagine that the white race, at least, would not acquiesce in this assumption. The argument also assumes that social prejudice may be overcome by legislation, and that equal rights cannot be secured to the Negro except by an enforced commingling of the two races. We cannot accept this proposition. If the two races are to meet upon terms of social equality, it must be the result of natural affinities, a mutual appreciation of each other's merits, and a voluntary consent of individuals. As was said by the Court of Appeals of New York in People *vs.* Gallagher, 93 N.Y. 438, 448, "This end can neither be accomplished nor promoted by laws which conflict with the general sentiment of the community upon whom they are designed to operate. When the government, therefore, has secured to each of its citizens equal rights before the law and equal opportunities for improvement and progress, it has accomplished the end for which it was organized and performed all of the functions respecting social advantages with which it is endowed." Legislation is powerless to eradicate racial instincts or to abolish distinctions based upon physical differences, and the attempt to do so can only result in accentuating the difficulties of the present situation. If the civil and political rights of both races be equal, one cannot be inferior to the other civilly or politically. If one race be inferior to the other socially, the Constitution of the United States cannot put them upon the same plane" (Plessy *vs.* Ferguson, 163 U.S. 537).

Limitations of space prevent repeating here all of this

great landmark decision. The down-to-earth common sense of this opinion completely destroys not only the unsupported reasoning of the present Court in the school cases but answers, many years in advance, the very arguments the present Court now relies upon.

Plessy *vs*. Ferguson does more. It castigates the current trend of the Court in arrogating to itself jurisdiction, in defiance of the Constitution, in such local matters as intrastate commerce, golf courses, theatres, swimming pools, etc. Perhaps we should not be surprised that the present Court found it necessary to "reject" Plessy *vs*. Ferguson.

HISTORY OF THE FOURTEENTH AMENDMENT

It will be observed from the last paragraph of the recent decision of the Supreme Court in the school cases, which we quoted, that the decision of that Court was predicated upon the idea that the segregation of races in the public schools violated the following language in the Fourteenth Amendment to the federal Constitution: "No State shall . . . deny to any person within its jurisdiction the equal protection of the laws."

We find some strange language in the Court's opinion on this subject. The Court says in effect that it has made a diligent and independent search and has asked for briefs upon the question, but that it cannot be determined with any degree of certainty just what the quoted portion of the constitutional amendment meant when it was passed.

If there is one subject that has been amply and fully explored in the great debates of American history and in every courtroom from border to border and coast to coast it has been the meaning of the wording of the Fourteenth Amendment. Most of it has to do with the due-process clause of the Fourteenth Amendment and not with the equal protection of the law, although there is much history upon the latter.

Immediately following the enactment of the Fourteenth Amendment, lawsuits began their way to the Supreme Court involving the application of this amendment to almost every phase of human conduct. One is certainly inclined to believe that the present Court overlooked a great many cases decided by the United States Supreme Court since 1868, many other federal cases, and a legion of constitutional and statutory provisions. We may be sure the Supreme Court could have had access to the great debates and other pertinent material referred to hereafter in the remarks of Senator Daniels. Could it be that the great weight of legal precedent was overwhelmingly opposed to the action contemplated by the Court? In considering this question all previous Courts had evolved a doctrine that has been long recognized as a correct and workable interpretation of the Constitution.

This is the doctrine of separate but equal rights as declared in the case of Plessy *vs.* Ferguson. The latter case was anchored upon the authority of previous cases of the Supreme Court of the United States involving constitutional provisions which are the same provisions involved here, and these decisions were rendered by jurists who were alive at the time of the passing of the Fourteenth Amendment to the Constitution; and being lawyers and judges at the time, their decisions based upon the meaning of the words of the Fourteenth Amendment would be far more persuasive than the overruling opinion of jurists who came upon the scene much later and who confessed that they could find little information or authority upon the subject.

It is obvious, as we shall show, that *there was and is an abundance of information available on the meaning of the Fourteenth Amendment. The Court would have none of it because it was in direct conflict with what the Court wanted the law to be.* Who, one may ask, was better qualified to speak on the meaning of the Fourteenth Amendment than the judges who were alive at the time of its passage and who, within the following thirty years, interpreted it?

On March 1, 1880, the Supreme Court of the United States handed down opinions in three cases: Strauder *vs.* West Virginia, 100 U.S. 664; State of Virginia *vs.* Rives, 100 U.S. 667; Ex Parte Commonwealth of Virginia *vs.* West Virginia, *vs.* J. D. Coles, 100 U.S. 677.

All of these cases involved an interpretation of the Fourteenth Amendment. These decisions followed so closely upon the adoption of that amendment that the Court in its opinions referred to it as "the recent amendment." These cases, and others cited herein, discussed in great detail the historic purposes and meaning of the language of the Fourteenth Amendment as it was understood at the time of its passage. These same cases, and many others, defined in indisputable terms the meaning of the words "equal protection of the laws," which meaning seemed to elude or confuse the present Court.

As later confirmed and immortalized in the decision of Plessy *vs.* Ferguson, all of these cases held that the meaning of the term "equal protection of the laws" was the usual and common-sense interpretation to be placed upon plain language. We have already referred to these principles briefly. They include:

1. Equal rights before the courts of this land.

2. Equal political rights, such as the right of elective franchise and the right to hold public office.

3. Economic rights, such as the right to acquire, hold, and convey property.

The necessary implications of these rights are readily understandable. They do not require psychiatric or sociological interpretation. They obviously do not refer to social conduct or local customs.

These cases uniformly held that the wording of the Fourteenth Amendment did not deprive the several States of the right to legislate upon such local and social problems as the segregation of races in schools and intrastate commerce. All Courts prior to the present one have adherred to these principles. Only the present Court seems to have overlooked Article 2 of the Fourteenth Amendment, which provided: "The Congress shall have power to enforce this article by appropriate legislation." Congress has enacted no law requiring the integration of races in schools, parks, theatres, swimming pools, or golf courses. If Congress had enacted such laws, they would certainly have been held invalid under the principle of the restraint of the powers of the federal government contained in the Tenth Amendment.

The statements by the Court that the meaning of the Fourteenth Amendment, at the time of its passage, was obscure and that the Court's investigation thereof was "inconclusive" are further refuted by a great mass of evidence.

Part of this evidence relates to the fact that the legislatures and the peoples of several of the States enacted laws or constitutional provisions providing for segregation in their public schools at the same time, or immediately after, ratifying the Fourteenth Amendment to the Constitution. Is it reasonable to assume that they would have done so had they believed that the Fourteenth Amendment prohibited such segregation? There appears no mention in the Court's opinion of these historic facts.

One fine illustration of the feelings and beliefs of the people of that day is contained in the history of the State of Tennessee. The last State to secede from the Union and the first to return, Tennessee was and is a southern State, but not part of what is known as the "Deep South." Its sympathies in the Civil War were divided between the two opposing forces. Tennessee ratified the Fourteenth Amendment to the Constitution of the United States on July 19, 1866. This amendment became part of the Constitution on the 28th of July, 1868. Its Constitutional Convention, held at Nashville, Tennessee on February 23, 1870, provided as follows in Section 12 of Article II of the Constitution of Tennessee:

Knowledge, learning, and virtue being essential to the preservation of republican institutions, and the diffusion of the opportunities and advantages of education throughout the different portions of the State being highly conducive to the promotion of this end, it shall be the duty of the General Assembly, in all future periods of this government, to cherish literature and science. . . . *No school established or aided under this Section shall allow*

*white and Negro children to be received as schol-
ars together in the same school.*

The foregoing, a constitutional provision, has never been amended, modified, or repealed. For 86 years it has been the fundamental law of the State. Similar situations exist in numerous other States. *The history of the Fourteenth Amendment and its interpretation at the time it passed is an open record for all to see who will read.*

FORMER DECISIONS OF THE SUPREME COURT

It is our purpose here not to lengthen unduly this discussion by a great volume of citations but rather refer to enough of them to indicate beyond question that the recent action of the Supreme Court of the United States was in many respects an unprecedented and unsupported venture entirely beyond the realm of anything that had ever been considered as legal reasoning.

On November 9, 1908, the Supreme Court of the United States handed down a published opinion styled Berea College *vs*. Kentucky, which is reported in 211 U.S. 45 and 29 S. Ct. 33. In that case, Berea College was being prosecuted for the violation of a Kentucky statute which prohibited the mixing or integration of races in the schools. The question was therefore presented directly to the Supreme Court of that day (November 9, 1908) as to the constitutionality of a State statute forbidding integration. The Kentucky statute was upheld. The Supreme Court's opinion mentions the Berea College case in its footnotes but does not comment upon it; presumably, it meant to reject it as it has rejected Plessy *vs*. Ferguson.

The Honorable Price Daniel, senator from Texas, on Tuesday, May 18, 1954, made a speech upon the floor of the Senate of the United States, which speech is contained in the *Congressional Record* of that date. He commented upon the legal questions involved in the decision of the Supreme Court of the previous day. Because the *Congressional Record* is not always readily available, and because Senator Daniel's remarks were so pertinent and authoritative, we quote from his remarks in the *Congressional Record*:

152

In Cumming *vs.* Board of Education (175 U.S. 528), decided in 1899, the Supreme Court said: "Under the circumstances disclosed, we cannot say that this action of the State court was, within the meaning of the Fourteenth Amendment, a denial by the State to the plaintiffs and to those associated with them of the equal protection of the laws or of any privilege belonging to them as citizens of the United States. We may add that while all admit that the benefits and burdens of public taxation must be shared by citizens without discrimination against any class on account of their race, the education of the people in schools maintained by State taxation is a matter belonging to the respective States, and *any interference on the part of federal authority with the management of such schools cannot be justified except in the case of a clear and unmistakable disregard of rights secured by the supreme law of the land.*"

The next case was that of Berea College *vs.* Kentucky (211 U.S. 45), decided in 1908, in which Justice Brewer said: "The single question for our consideration is whether . . . a statute providing that there should not be commingling of the races in a private college . . . conflicts with the federal Constitution. . . . That the legislature of Kentucky desired to separate the teaching of white and colored children may be conceded."

The Supreme Court upheld the statute of Kentucky in that case.

The next case which passed on this point was the Supreme Court case of Gong Lum *vs.* Rice (275 U.S. 78), decided in 1927, a case directly in point. The pertinent portion of the Constitution of Mississippi, as set out in the Court's opinion, reads as follows: "Separate schools shall be maintained for children of the white and colored races."

A Chinese girl, classified as "colored" under the Mississippi law, was denied admission to the white schools. A direct attack was made on the constitutionality of the separation of the races for schooling purposes, the contention being made that such was a violation of the equal-protection clause of the Fourteenth Amendment.

In its opinion yesterday the Supreme Court disagreed with the statement I have just made. I wish to quote from the Supreme Court's opinion of yesterday concerning the 1927 case of Gong Lum against Rice, as follows: "The validity of the doctrine . . . of separate but equal . . . was not challenged."

To those who hear or who will read these remarks, I leave judgment as to the accuracy of that statement. The first assignment of error in the Gong Lum against Rice case was as follows: "A child of school age and otherwise qualified . . . is denied the equal protection of the laws when she is excluded from such schools solely on the ground that she is a Chinese child and not of the Caucasian race."

Mr. Justice Taft, speaking for a unanimous Court composed of himself and Justices Holmes, Van Devanter, Brandeis, Stone, McReynolds, Sutherland, Butler, and Sanford, clearly stated the question before the Court in these words: "The case then reduces itself to the question whether a State can be said to afford to a child of Chinese ancestry, born in this country and a citizen of the United States, equal protection of the laws by giving her the opportunity for a common school education in a school which receives only colored children."

This shows that the Court was especially concerned with the separation of children in schools under the equal-protection clause.

Mr. Justice Taft said: "We cannot say that this action . . . was, within the meaning of the Fourteenth Amendment, a denial . . . of the equal process of the laws. . . . The education of the people in schools maintained by State taxation is a matter belonging to the respective States."

The opinion by the Supreme Court, concurred in by such Justices as Holmes and Brandeis, went on to say: "In Plessy *vs*. Ferguson . . . in upholding the validity under the Fourteenth Amendment of a statute of Louisiana requiring the separation of the white and colored in railway coaches, a more difficult question than this, this Court, speaking of permitting race separation, said: 'The most common instance of this is connected with the establishment of separate schools for white and colored children, which has been held to be a valid exercise of the legislative power even by the courts of States where the political rights of the colored race have been longest and most earnestly enforced.' "

The Chief Justice, speaking for the Court, said: *"We think that it is the same question which has been many times decided to be within the constitutional power of the State legislatures to settle without intervention of the federal courts under the federal Constitution."*

The Court concluded: *"The right and power of the State to regulate the method of providing for the education of its youth at public expense is clear. . . .* The decision is within the discretion of the State in regulating its public schools and does not conflict with the Fourteenth Amendment. The judgment of the Supreme Court of Mississippi is affirmed."

As I have said, there is a total of at least thirteen federal court decisions which follow these Supreme Court cases holding that separate but equal

facilities do not violate the Fourteenth Amendment. . . ."

The senator then put into the *Congressional Record* the
list of thirteen other federal court decisions supporting his
statement. He further placed in the record of that date an
extremely well-prepared table showing fifty-nine State and
territorial court decisions upholding the "separate-but-equal
doctrine" as valid under the Fourteenth Amendment of the
Constitution. In addition to this valuable table there is also
contained in this issue of the *Record* excerpts from the brief
submitted by the attorneys general of seventeen States in
the case of Sweatt *vs.* Painter to which we have referred.
All these references are too long to include in an ordinary
discussion of segregation or integration, but the thoughtful
student, the lawyer, the statesman, or the individual who is
sufficiently interested in the welfare of his country to consider this vital problem upon its history and its merits would
do well to obtain a copy of the *Congressional Record* and
of these references.

We have noted that the Supreme Court, in the opinion
in the Brown case, confessed its inability to ascertain the
intent of the Fourteenth Amendment at the time of its
passage. Senator Russell of Georgia speaking in the
Senate on Tuesday, May 18, 1954, as quoted in the *Congressional Record,* had this to say with reference to that
portion of the Court's opinion:

> The able senator from Texas has read from the
> decision the statement that the members of the
> Court were unable to ascertain the intention of
> those who proposed, as well as those who adopted,
> the Fourteenth Amendment. The Court not only
> stated that the intent at the time was inconclusive,
> but the clear influence of the decision is that it is
> hardly worthy of consideration by this Court.

Mr. President, if there has been a cardinal rule of construction since the dawn of Anglo-Saxon justice—until this decision which undertakes to brush it aside—it is that the intent of the lawmaker was of vital importance in arriving at the proper construction of statutes. The case to which the senator from Texas refers also shows that heretofore the Courts have thought it to be their duty to examine the intent in construing the application and meaning of the Constitution of the United States and its amendments. . . .

The history of the Fourteenth Amendment makes it perfectly clear to any fair-minded man of reasonable intelligence that neither the Congress which submitted the amendment nor the legislative bodies of the States that ratified it ever dreamed it would apply to, and justify, the decision in the separate-schools case. The very Congress which proposed the Fourteenth Amendment provided for the adoption of a separate school system for the races in the District of Columbia. My own State at the time had a legislature that was largely carpetbagger or scalawag. The same legislature which ratified the Fourteenth Amendment proposed by the Congress wrote a constitution for the State of Georgia which contained a provision for separate schools. I do not see how anyone who pretends to understand the English language, who has really made a study of the subject, could have failed to ascertain the intent of all of those who are responsible for the Fourteenth Amendment now being a part of the Constitution.

In support of Senator Russell's statement, Senator Price Daniel said:

I wish to say that at the time when I was handling a case on this issue before the Supreme Court, as attorney general of Texas, I had occasion to read all the debates that occurred in Congress at the time of the submission of the Fourteenth Amendment and also all the debates in the State legislatures which were available. I went thoroughly into the matter. I have before me approximately 100 pages of extracts from the arguments and the record of the action of Congress and the action taken by State legislatures. I did not find one indication that any member of Congress or any of the State legislators felt that the adoption of the Fourteenth Amendment would prohibit separate schools, if they were equal. On the contrary, many indications are to be found, including the passage by the Congress and by the State legislatures of legislation for separate schools, that separate schools were permitted under the Fourteenth Amendment, if they were equal.

"THE REASONING OF THE COURT"

Besides abandoning the rule of *stare decisis,* the Supreme Court, in the integration case, indulged in language and conclusions which are strange indeed. Let us notice just a few of them briefly. We quote from The Opinion: "Does segregation of children in the public schools solely on the basis of race, even though the physical facilities and other 'tangible' factors may be equal, deprive the children of the minority group of equal additional opportunities? We believe that it does."

The foregoing is not a conclusion of law but a conclusion as to a psychological situation. Unless the authority for it is contained in the textbooks shortly to be discussed, there appears no such authority except dictum in the cases of Sweatt *vs.* Painter, and McLaurin *vs.* Oklahoma State Regents, 339 U.S. 629 and 637. These cases were decided by the Supreme Court when its personnel consisted of a majority of those still on the Supreme Court. In other words, the Court was simply citing, in referring to these cases, statements made by the same Court in former opinions.

The Court's finding of alleged fact, apparently, is founded upon no proof, but actually is contrary to the experiences of southern schools for many years.

The language of the questioned findings discloses that it is sheer sophistry. Note that the opinion says that it "deprives the children of minority groups of equal educational opportunities." Within the Mississippi Delta, in Southern Mississippi, Alabama, Georgia, in most of rural South Carolina and Louisiana, the "minority group" will be composed of white children. Due to the great preponderance of the Negro population in many of these rural counties, the Negro

159

children will greatly outnumber the whites. Does the Supreme Court therefore intend to say that segregated schools deprive the white children, definitely the minority group there, of equal educational opportunities?

The words imply that the little Negro children, who constitute a majority, so far as many rural southern schools are concerned, are denied this fictional equal opportunity because nationally they constitute a "minority party." If the latter is true, we wonder how the little Negro children in the South come to the realization at such a tender age that they are part of a minority group.

Further in its opinion, the Court said, referring to Negro children in grade and high school: "To separate them from others of similar age and qualifications solely because of their race generates a feeling of inferiority as to their status in the community that may affect their hearts and minds in a way unlikely ever to be undone." It would be interesting indeed to know upon what statement of facts the Court based this gem. *This same argument was made before the Supreme Court in the case of Plessy vs. Ferguson. The Court, at that time, ridiculed and rejected this fallacious argument in language which we have quoted.*

The tender solicitude of the Court for "the hearts and minds" of children suffering from segregation on account of race, probably regarded by some as evidence of what has been loosely called "humanitarianism," could not arise to any greater dignity than the authority from which it sprang. There were certainly no proven facts to justify the quoted finding, and it is certainly repudiated by the declared law upon the subject. The Court did not say—but we will assume—that the damage to the "hearts and minds" of these little children is supposedly restricted to children of the Negro race. Or, could it be that the Supreme Court is saying that white children of the South suffer irreparable damage to their "hearts and minds" and acquire a feeling of inferiority because they are required to attend a school composed of white children only? The children of the

South have known only segregated schools. In many respects, the sociological reasoning of the opinion is more amazing than its legal aspects.

The Court had already found that the facilities for the separate races were equal, and the only reason advanced for holding that segregation deprived the Negro children of equal educational opportunities was that such segregation was based upon racial differences. This opinion completely overlooks the fact that there are many differences besides the difference in color. We cannot help wondering why the Supreme Court would not take into consideration, as former courts had done, some of the factors which we have already mentioned, including the difference in standards of living between the white and Negro children in a majority of communities in the South.

Did the Court consider the disparity of school advancement between the Negro children and white children of similar ages? We wonder if the Court weighed the psychological trauma of the Negro students finding that they were placed in segregated schools with children of their own race against the psychological trauma which would follow by comparison of their standard of living, their advancement in school, and their racial differences that must appear before their eyes daily when forced into integration in white schools where they do not want to go and where the white people do not want them to go. The Supreme Court decision cannot have the effect of changing the "standards of living" nor of reversing the history and traditions of the last hundred years. Until these conditions are reversed, and until the standards of living are more nearly equalized, it seems obvious that the psychological trauma suffered by Negro children as a result of forced integration will be far greater than the psychological trauma of continuing segregation in the public schools as it has been carried on ever since the beginning of the school systems in the South.

It should not be overlooked that the white children of the South, who, as has been stated before, will often be the "minority group," will also suffer great psychological trauma when forced into integrated schools in violation of their customs and accepted way of life. The Court's decision suggests no remedy for the damage that may result to "their hearts and minds."

The unsupported findings of the Court are based upon intangible rather than tangible factors. Intangibles have been described as "a nonexistent state of affairs about which everybody knows nothing." When the Court abandoned legal precedent for intangible considerations, it wandered far afield into the realm of speculation. Such speculation is unknown to the law and inconsistent with the Anglo-Saxon theory of jurisprudence. The departure by the Court from the time-honored rule, from the precedent of established law and proven fact into the realm of adjudication upon intangible consideration, is even more startling when we consider the source of the authorities which the High Court found so persuasive.

UPON WHAT AUTHORITIES DID THE COURT RELY?

We now come to what is perhaps the most astounding statement to be found in the printed opinion of any court. In this statement we find verification of all that we have said regarding the philosophy of the Court and the authority upon which it relies.

That statement is as follows: *"Whatever may be the extent of psychological knowledge at the time of Plessy* vs. *Ferguson, this finding is amply supported by modern authorities."* We will deal with this sentence in two parts. The first part throws great light upon the frame of mind of the Court in the intimation that, in view of modern psychological knowledge, the accumulation of wisdom, knowledge, and learning by the human race for 5,000 years prior to and including the time of Plessy *vs.* Ferguson is as nothing compared to modern "authorities." Many of us will hesitate to disdain the philosophical, literary, and governmental attainments of men like Plato, Aristotle, Benjamin Franklin, William Shakespeare, and Thomas Jefferson in order to pay tribute to these modern authorities.

Let us consider the last part of the quoted sentence: "This finding is amply supported by modern authorities." The findings referred to are those that we have quoted above. They may be termed the sociological reason for forced integration of the races in southern schools. What are these modern authorities on the basis of which the Supreme Court abandons the wealth of legal precedents which we have cited and for which it has ignored or violated the Tenth Amendment to our Constitution and the constitutions and segregation laws of sixteen "sovereign States" of the Union? The answer to that question reveals a situation so

163

inherently dangerous and detrimental to our basic laws and to every concept of jurisprudence that the reader might well cry out in anguish, as a member of the Supreme Court once did: "The Constitution is gone!"

The authorities cited by the Supreme Court in support of the statement which we have quoted are set out in Footnote 11 to the Court's opinion; and in order that there be no mistake we quote here the footnote in full:

> K. B. Clark, *Effect of Prejudice and Discrimination on Personality Development* (Midcentury White House Conference on Children and Youth, 1950); Witmer and Kotinsky, *Personality in the Making* (1952), c. VI; Deutscher and Chein, *The Psychological Effects of Enforced Segregation: A Survey of Social Science Opinion,* 26 J Psychol. 259 (1948); Chein, *What Are the Psychological Effects of Segregation Under Conditions of Equal Facilities?* 3 Int. J. Opinion and Attitude Res. 229 (1949); Brameld, *Educational Costs,* in *Discrimination and National Welfare* (MacIver, ed. 1949), 44-48; Frazier, *The Negro in the United States* (1949), 674-681. And see generally, Myrdal, *An American Dilemma* (1944).

It will be observed that the foregoing list of modern authorities contains not a single constitutional provision, no statute, no decision of any court—in fact, no authority which could be accepted by any court as a legal precedent.

We will refer a little bit later to the Senate resolution introduced by Senator Eastland. In a speech on the floor of the United States Senate on Thursday, May 26, 1955, Senator Eastland delivered a learned address in which he read the pedigrees of all these so-called authorities. A brief reference to them will indicate the terrible danger involved in accepting them as authorities.

The first authority, K. B. Clark, a Negro, is a professional social-science expert employed by the N.A.A.C.P. whose lawyer argued the school cases before the Supreme Court. *It is certainly astounding that a court would accept as persuasive authority a paper written by a non-legal employee of a party interested in the outcome of the litigation.*

Another authority, Theodore Brameld, was shown to be a member of at least ten communist-tinted organizations and a man whose name appeared in a very favorable light in the *Daily Worker.*

Franklin Frazier, according to the senator, has a record before the Committee of Un-American Activities of the United States House of Representatives, showing eighteen connections with communist causes in the United States.

According to the footnote, the Court adopted generally as its leading authority Myrdal's book *An American Dilemma.* Myrdal was brought to this country by the Carnegie Foundation from the University of Stockholm.

Senator Eastland says: "He noted himself a social engineer. He was a socialist who had served the communist cause. He admitted he had no knowledge of the Negro question in the United States." The senator proceeds to show that Myrdal advised and associated with the leading communist sympathizers and communist organizers while in this country. Myrdal's writings show absolute contempt for the Constitution of the United States, calling that document "nearly a fraud upon the people."

How did these questionable nonlegal writings become a part of the school-integration cases? They were not introduced as evidence in the trial of the cases. They were not competent evidence. They were not such "authorities" as courts will consider in a legal brief. They had the sanction of no constitution, nor of the written or common law. They did not represent the pronouncement of any judicial tribunal. They were not subject to cross-examination by the defendants to determine either the truth of, or the motive for, their statements. Their inclusion as a basis for the

Court's "findings" cannot be justified upon any theory known to American jurisprudence.

As a nation, we have always considered our courts bound by the written and established law. After hearing all the evidence that may be properly introduced, and after considering such evidence in the light of established laws, the courts make their "findings." The findings of the Supreme Court in the school-integration cases rested neither upon established law, nor upon proven fact. In fact, the opinion ignored both.

The only authority referred to by the Court as the basis for its findings came from the textbook writings which, for the reasons suggested above, should not have been considered by the Court for any purpose. There is no precedent for the action of the Supreme Court in plucking out of thin air such incompetent and inadmissible evidence and using it as the weapon to overthrow a century of established law. If this course is to be followed, then our law ceases to be an established and dependable bulwark of government and becomes a vagrant philosophy colored only by writers who may happen to appeal to the fancy of the court.

The question recurs: how did these writings, which the Court accepted as authority, become a part of the cases so that they could be considered by the Court? Not one of the writings possessed any qualification entitling it to be considered by the Court as authority. If these writings were not introduced as evidence, and if they could not be submitted to, nor received by, the Court as legal authority, there was no way by which the Court could legally consider or take notice of them.

Furthermore, if the writers themselves had been called as witnesses to appear in person in the trial court and to testify, such evidence would have been incompetent and would have been excluded by the Court upon objection. We may be certain that such objection would have been made.

Furthermore, if such witnesses had been called, and had

been permitted to testify, there could be little doubt that their testimony would have been impeached by a multitude of character witnesses. If we assume that their testimony could have been admitted under any rule of law, the defendants would have had a legal right to introduce witnesses to refute such testimony.

If these writers had testified to the same philosophy as expressed in their textbooks, we are still faced with the reality that the defendants in the integration cases could and would have produced a multitude of qualified witnesses of outstanding integrity and ability, of unimpeachable character and patriotism, and thoroughly familiar with the issues, who would have overwhelmingly refuted the testimony of these "authorities."

It was upon such authority that the Supreme Court "rejected Plessy *vs.* Ferguson." It was obvious to either a lawyer or a layman that if the courts of this nation resort to deciding lawsuits and interpreting the Constitution on the basis of what some psychiatrist or textbook writer says rather than upon the time-honored precedent of Constitution and established laws, no person's property or liberty is safe. Authorities could be found in textbooks for almost any and all theories and beliefs, regardless of how profound or how inane. Anybody with sufficient time, writing material, and money can publish a book on any subject. Psychology and psychiatry, no doubt, have a place in education and the treatment of the mentally and physically sick; but if we accept psychology textbooks as the final authority in the fundamental laws of the land, there would be little necessity for studying the law. Instead one would merely search for a writer who could provide the "lawyer" with a textbook agreeable with his particular beliefs or needs of the moment.

We have referred to the statement by Senator Russell on the Court's decision with reference to the Fourteenth Amendment. He also had something very interesting to say about the substitution of a psychologist as an authority in-

168 The AGE of ERROR

stead of the general and long-honored practice of citing legal precedents.

The decision of the Supreme Court was unique in other respects. Not only did the opinion reverse the construction of the Constitution which had been applied by the Supreme Court at a time when there were able lawyers and experienced members sitting on the Supreme Court; not only did the opinion strike down all the precedents on the subject and also State constitutions; but, for the first time, the Court admittedly substituted psychology for law and precedents when it came to construing the Constitution of the United States.

It is my opinion that if the Supreme Court is to abandon law and precedents in favor of psychology in arriving at its opinions, the rights of the States which might remain or the liberties of the American people should not be subjected to the findings of amateur psychologists whose chief background and experience has been in the field of practical politics and not in either law or psychology. If they are to rely on psychology, then we should either add trained psychologists of recognized ability to the Court, or else we should provide that a Court psychologist of high standing shall attend the sessions of the Court and assist the Attorney General of the United States in bringing the Court to its conclusions.

The dangers alluded to are neither fanciful nor remote. The danger seems to have been encountered in the present case, the very first one in which radical departure of authority was attempted. On May 26, 1955, Senator James O. Eastland of Mississippi introduced to the Senate a resolution (S. Res. 104) which is as follows:

RESOLUTION

WHEREAS, the Supreme Court of the United States rendered a decision on May 17, 1954, in the case of Brown *et al.*, and four related cases, which admittedly departed from the established law and precedents in declaring the "separate but equal" doctrine of separation of the white and black races was unconstitutional insofar as it applied to public school facilities; and,

WHEREAS, This decision was based solely and alone on psychological, sociological, and anthropological considerations, in that the Court states: "Whatever may have been the extent of psychological knowledge at the time of Plessy *vs.* Ferguson, this finding is amply supported by modern authority"; and,

WHEREAS, The footnote to the opinion lists six allegedly modern authorities and concludes with the sentence: "And see generally Myrdal, *An American Dilemma* (1944)"; and,

WHEREAS, A provisional investigation of the authorities upon which the Supreme Court relied reveals to a shocking degree their connection with and participation in the world-wide communist conspiracy, in that Brameld and Frazier, listed in the group of six authorities, have no less than 28 citations in the files of the Committee on Un-American Activities of the United States House of Representatives revealing membership in, or participation with, communist or communist-front organizations and activities; and,

WHEREAS, The book, *An American Dilemma,* was prepared by a Swedish socialist who declared in the book that the United States Constitution was "impractical and unsuited to modern conditions" and its adoption was "nearly a plot against the common people"; and,

WHEREAS, This book was the result of collaboration between Myrdal and certain alleged "scholars and experts" assigned him by the Carnegie Corp., of Alger Hiss fame; and,

WHEREAS, Sixteen of these so-called scholars and experts, who contributed to no less than 272 different articles and portions of the book, have been cited numerous times as members of communist and subversive organizations; and,

WHEREAS, The citation of these authorities clearly indicates a dangerous influence and control exerted on the Court by communist-front pressure groups and other enemies of the American republic and individual members thereof that is inimical to the general welfare and best interest of the republic; and,

WHEREAS, This Senate, the 16 sovereign States whose constitutions were nullified by the illegal decision of the Supreme Court, and all of the people of the United States are now entitled to know beyond doubt and peradventure the complete extent and degree of communist and communist-front activity and influence in the preparation of the psuedo "modern scientific authority" which was the sole and only basis for the decision of the Supreme Court: Now, therefore, be it

RESOLVED, That it is the sense of the Senate that the Senate Committee on the Judiciary should proceed under its presently constituted powers to investigate the extent and degree of participation by individuals and groups identified with the communist conspiracy, communist-front organizations, and alien ideologies in the formation of the "modern scientific authority" upon which the Supreme Court relied in the school-integration cases.

In support of his resolution, Senator Eastland said:

> The Court has not only arrogated to itself powers which were not delegated to it under the Constitution of the United States and has entered the fields of the legislative and executive branches of the government, but they are attempting to graft into the organic law of the land the teachings, preachments, and social doctrines arising from a political philosophy which is the antithesis of the principles upon which this government was founded. The origin of the doctrines can be traced to Karl Marx, and their propagation is part and parcel of the conspiracy to divide and destroy this government through internal controversy. The Court adopts this propaganda as "modern scientific authority."

No Precedent Except in Russia

Mr. President, in the long legal history of this country there has never before been a time when an appellate court or Supreme Court of the United States relied solely and alone on scientific authority to sustain a legal decision. I am informed that in the long history of British jurisprudence there has never been a time when the high courts of England have resorted to such dubious authority, but that their decisions have been based on the law. Mr. President, my information is that the one time when the high appellate court of any major western nation has resorted to textbooks and the works of agitators to sustain its decision was when the high court of Germany sustained Hitler's racist laws.

What the Bar and the people of the United States are slow to realize is that in the rendition of the opinion on the school-segregation cases the en-

tire basis of American jurisprudence was swept
away. There is only one other comparable system
of jurisprudence which is based upon the winds of
vacillating, political, and pseudo-scientific opinion
—the Peoples Court of Soviet Russia. In that vast
vacuum of liberty, the basis of their jurisprudence
is the vacillating, ever changing winds of pseudo-
authority. And that today is the basis of American
jurisprudence as announced by a unanimous opinion of our Supreme Court.

Senator Eastland then presented a bill of particulars in
which he discussed the writers who were mentioned by the
Supreme Court in its opinion as authority for its decision.
His indictment of them connects many of these writers
with some communist-front or subversive organization or
activity. Senator Eastland's charges were made on the floor
of the Senate in great detail almost a year ago. If these
charges had been unfounded or untrue, it would certainly
appear reasonable that they would have been met and refuted before this. If they are true, we have the very sad but
convincing proof that the communist cause works in mysterious ways its wonders to perform. It can hardly be denied
that the communist cause has seemed to have some mystic
appeal to many people in our colleges and universities.
Communists are also prolific writers and, apparently, very
persuasive.

No lawyer could conceive of a greater disaster that could
befall us than to have our splendid system of jurisprudence, which with all its faults is unquestionably the best
on earth, supplanted by the theories of textbook writers on
psychology and psychiatry, be they communist or otherwise.

THE SOUTHERN MANIFESTO

Our federal government, by constitutional provision, is divided into three sections: legislative, executive and judicial. There have been comparatively few instances in our history when either the executive or legislative branch of the government publicly and seriously challenged the judiciary, or to be more specific, the Supreme Court, which is regarded as the fountainhead of the judicial department. There have been few such occasions, and they have generally marked turning points in our history.

For the most part, members of the Senate and the House of Representatives are, or have been, lawyers. Lawyers like to believe in the infallibility of the Supreme Court. It is a sad day indeed when a lawyer, who by law is an officer of the court, loses faith in either the ability or integrity of a court of last resort. Such courts have generally been held in very high esteem, and lawyers want to believe that the Supreme Court will always remain as the last bulwark of our freedom.

For these reasons the action of certain members of Congress in publishing what has been known as the "Southern Manifesto" assumes great significance. Most of these gentlemen were trained lawyers and patriotic statesmen.

On March 12, 1956, the venerable Senator George, of Georgia, presented to the Senate of the United States what has been referred to as the "Manifesto" and which was titled, "Declaration of Constitutional Principles." This declaration is contained in the *Congressional Record* of that date and was signed by nineteen senators representing eleven States and by seventy-seven members of the House of Representatives. As Senator George stated, the Declaration had not

173

been hastily conceived but had been carefully considered by members of the Senate for several weeks. This very grave and important document is as follows:

A DECLARATION OF PRINCIPLES

The unwarranted decision of the Supreme Court in the public-school cases is now bearing the fruit always produced when men substitute naked power for established law.

The Founding Fathers gave us a Constitution of checks and balances because they realized the inescapable lesson of history that no man or group of men can be safely entrusted with unlimited power. They framed this Constitution with its provisions for change by amendment in order to secure the fundamentals of government against the dangers of temporary popular passion or the personal predilections of public officeholders.

We regard the decision of the Supreme Court in the school cases as a clear abuse of judicial power. It climaxes a trend in the federal judiciary undertaking to legislate, in derogation of the authority of Congress, and to encroach upon the reserved rights of the States and the people.

The original Constitution does not mention education. Neither does the Fourteenth Amendment nor any other amendment. The debates preceding the submission of the Fourteenth Amendment clearly show that there was no intent that it should affect the system of education maintained by the States.

The very Congress which proposed the amendment subsequently provided for segregated schools in the District of Columbia.

When the amendment was adopted in 1868, there were thirty-seven States of the Union.

Every one of the twenty-six States that had any substantial racial differences among its people either approved the operation of segregated schools already in existence or subsequently established such schools by action of the same lawmaking body which considered the Fourteenth Amendment.

As admitted by the Supreme Court in the public-school case (Brown *vs.* Board of Education), the doctrine of separate but equal schools "apparently originated in Robert *vs.* City of Boston 1849), upholding school segregation against attack as being violative of a State constitutional guarantee of equality." This constitutional doctrine began in the North, not in the South, and it was followed not only in Massachusetts, but in Connecticut, New York, Illinois, Indiana, Michigan, Minnesota, New Jersey, Ohio, Pennslyvania, and other northern States until they, exercising their rights as States through the constitutional processes of local self-government, changed their school systems.

In the case of Plessy *vs.* Ferguson in 1896, the Supreme Court expressly declared that under the Fourteenth Amendment no person was denied any of his rights if the States provided separate but equal public facilities. This decision has been followed in many other cases. It is notable that the Supreme Court, speaking through Chief Justice Taft, a former President of the United States, unanimously declared in 1927 in Lum *vs.* Rice that the "separate but equal" principle is "within the discretion of the State in regulating its public schools and does not conflict with the Fourteenth Amendment."

This interpretation, restated time and again, became a part of the life of the people of many of the States and confirmed their habits, customs, traditions, and way of life. It is founded on elemental humanity and common sense, for parents should not be deprived by government of the right to direct the lives and education of their own children.

Though there has been no constitutional amendment or act of Congress changing this established legal principle almost a century old, the Supreme Court of the United States, with no legal basis for such action, undertook to exercise their naked judicial power and substituted their personal political and social ideas for the established law of the land.

This unwarranted exercise of power by the Court, contrary to the Constitution, is creating chaos and confusion in the States principally affected. It is destroying the amicable relations between the white and Negro races that have been created through ninety years of patient effort by the good people of both races. It has planted hatred and suspicion where there has been heretofore friendship and understanding.

Without regard to the consent of the governed, outside agitators are threatening immediate and revolutionary changes in our public-school systems. If done, this is certain to destroy the system of public education in some of the States.

With the gravest concern for the explosive and dangerous condition created by this decision and inflamed by outside meddlers:

We reaffirm our reliance on the Constitution as the fundamental law of the land.

We decry the Supreme Court's encroachments on rights reserved to the States and to the people, contrary to established law and to the Constitution.

We commend the motives of those States which have declared the intention to resist forced integration by any lawful means.

We appeal to the States and people who are not directly affected by these decisions to consider the constitutional principles involved against the time when they too, on issues vital to them, may be the victims of judicial encroachment.

Even though we constitute a minority in the present Congress, we have full faith that a majority of the American people believe in the dual system of government which has enabled us to achieve our greatness and will in time demand that the reserved rights of the States and of the people be made secure against judicial usurpation.

We pledge ourselves to use all lawful means to bring about a reversal of this decision which is contrary to the Constitution and to prevent the use of force in its implementation.

In this trying period, as we all seek to right this wrong, we appeal to our people not to be provoked by the agitators and troublemakers invading our States and to scrupulously refrain from disorder and lawless acts.

WHERE DO WE GO FROM HERE?

Under the present Supreme Court decisions, it is obvious that there will be a strong effort to deprive all States of federal financial assistance if those States do not follow the philosophy of the Supreme Court in the matter of integration. This intention has already been abundantly manifested. There is no reason to suppose that the financial aid to be withheld would be restricted to matters pertaining to education. It would be just as reasonable to suppose that federal aid for highways would be denied to those States having segregation laws or permitting segregation in public conveyances upon the State highways. Federal aid could be denied to cities which permit segregation of the races in theatres, streetcars, or recreational facilities.

Since the N.A.A.C.P. avows that one of its purposes in the school-integration fight is to achieve "full integration," and since this undoubtedly means an effort to remove all bans on intermarriage, it is quite obvious that one of the next moves will be directed toward destroying the laws against miscegenation. Certainly these agitators will not be satisfied with having won only one of their declared objectives.

In view of the Court's opinion in the integration cases, we can speculate on what its opinion would be in a case brought before it involving a State law against racial intermarriage. If, as the Court has held, the Fourteenth Amendment prohibits all States from passing or enforcing laws requiring segregation of the races in public schools, would not that same reasoning dictate that the same amendment prohibits the passage or enforcement of laws against intermarriage? If laws prohibiting integration of the races in the

178

schools are held to violate the "equal-protection-of-the-laws" provision, it seems to follow that the same Court, using the same reasoning, would hold that laws prohibiting miscegenation violated the same provision of the Constitution. Both laws are designed to create classifications based alone upon color. If State laws were stricken down, then the federal government, speaking through its Supreme Court, could refuse to recognize the validity for any purpose (such as tax purposes) of marriages solemnized in a State having constitutional or statutory prohibitions against intermarriage.

There would be only one step further to conceive of a court "order" that a certain percentage of the marriages solemnized in any State should be racially intermixed, based upon a formula prorated as to the percentages of the population of the Negroes and whites within that State. Far-fetched? Not any more than the opinion of the Supreme Court in the school-integration cases would have appeared had it been made before the advent of the present Court. When once the "fence is jumped," there is no restraining force.

The inescapable conclusion is that the present trend of the Supreme Court must be stopped. Merely stopping the trend, however, will not suffice. Many of its decisions must be rejected or reversed if our constitutional form of government is to survive. The only way to preserve our constitutional freedoms inviolate is to remove from our declared and reported interpretations of the Constitution the blight of these erroneous decisions. Opinions of the Supreme Court nullifying the State laws and constitutions, striking at the very heart of local government, based upon incompetent or nonexistent evidence and supported only by the writings of misinformed and misguided agitators, must be repudiated by the High Court as well as by the people.

These unsupported and unconstitutional opinions of the Supreme Court do not deal entirely with segregation or racial questions. They're spreading now into every field of government. First, they appeared as a gentle breeze. Now they are reaching the proportions of a tornado. As an illustration, there is the case of Harry Slochower, an employee of the New York City Board of Education, who was fired by the board because he refused to answer questions by a Senate sub-committee concerning his communist activities. He refused to answer on Fifth-Amendment grounds, claiming that his answer might tend to incriminate him. The Supreme Court held that New York, which had acted in accordance with its charter, had violated Slochower's constitutional privileges. The Court also held on April 2, 1956, that the State of Pennsylvania could not enact valid laws on the subject of sedition. About four weeks later, it reversed the court of appeals for the District of Columbia in a case wherein the court had required the Communist party to register in accordance with the laws on subversive-activity control and communist control. Here we have a striking example of the Court's unlawful assumption of power in its unwillingness to permit city, State, or federal laws to eliminate the treasonable activity of the only enemy in this world which might be capable of, and is interested in, destroying the United States—the Communist party. There can be little doubt that these opinions gave much aid and comfort to that enemy.

Since the trend appears to be continuing and becoming more flagrant in disregard of constitutional restraints, we must ask ourselves the question: "Where do we go from here?"

WHAT IS THE SOLUTION?

We will consider briefly some possible "legal means" mentioned in the Declaration. Methods of combatting the obvious error of the Supreme Court will suggest themselves as time passes. One or more of these methods may work. A lawyer's suggestion might well be to keep presenting the question to the Supreme Court, supported by proof as to the facts, substantiated by authority as to the law, and fortified by the strongest arguments and references as to the weakness of the authorities used by the Supreme Court in support of its last opinion. We can hope that when these facts are developed and the law fully discussed, that this Court, or a subsequent Court, will see the error of its way and reject the decision based upon the textbook writings of individuals, whether reds, whites, or blacks, and reverse the ruling in the case of Brown *vs.* Board of Education of Topeka, as well as in associated cases.

This crisis precipitated by the recent trend of the Court's opinions may also serve to engender more care in the nominating, advising, and consenting to the appointment of justices of the High Court. Perhaps the public forgets that these are usually political appointments, dictated many times by geographical location, party affiliation, or political expediency.

Yet these nine men, appointed for life, constitute a court from which there is no appeal. Justices so appointed may have little or no judicial experience, although they sit in judgment upon appeals from district or appellate Courts composed of judges who may be far better trained at the bar and on the bench. Only three members of the present Court had any previous judicial experience, and some of

181

them had little or no experience as lawyers practicing their profession at the bar.

We have become so accustomed to accepting as final the decisions of government and of the courts that the illusion has developed that such decisions are sacred and inviolate. The popular conception seems to be that, once an individual is clothed in the black robes of the Supreme Court, he thereby acquires all of the facilities and abilities consonant with his position.

Two neighbors were discussing the beliefs of their respective churches. One said, "My church believes that all ministers of our faith should be educated before being licensed to preach."

Her neighbor replied, "We do not have that belief. We believe that when a man is 'called to preach,' at the same time he receives the knowledge of how to preach."

We may lose our most treasured possessions if we adopt the belief that anyone appointed by a President to the Supreme Court of the United States receives at the same time a knowledge fitting him to perform the duties of that great office.

The student of our judicial history is faced with the realization that appointments to the Supreme Court for the last generation have often tended away from proven judicial ability and toward political and sociological considerations. When a Court so composed, or any court, assumes powers never granted to it by the Constitution or by the people, the results may be catastrophic. Such assumed or arrogated powers, if not curbed, inevitably result in a government of men and not of law. Such government is dictatorship, the form of a totalitarian state. The responsibility for the Supreme Court rests squarely upon the President and the Senate, which advises and consents to such appointments.

Recently there have appeared appeals to the people to "respect" or "uphold" the Supreme Court. These appeals obviously refer to criticism directed at the Court on account of its current trend. Such appeals overlook the basic truths concerning our whole system of government. The Court should be—and is—respected as an institution. The judges composing the Supreme Court are entitled to respect and support only to the extent that their opinions are just, wise, and constitutional. It is not the duty of anyone to "uphold" the Court. Rather it is the duty of all to "uphold" our Constitution and established legal principles. In a constitutional crisis, persons, as individuals, may be expendable, but the constitutional principles of government are never expendable.

Senator Russell, on March 15, 1955, in speaking to the Senate upon the appointment of Mr. Justice Harlan, said: "I have become increasingly concerned over the appointment to the highest Court of this land, a Court from whose decisions there is no appeal, of those who have had no judicial experience whatever or such limited judicial experience that it has not grown into the maturity which comes from long service on the bench. There are other qualifications for service on the Supreme Court of the United States than mere brilliance of intellect or power of advocacy at the bar. The maturity of a real judge derives from judicial experience and judicial restraint. The willingness to decide questions as the judge finds the law to be, rather than to attempt to write the law as the judge feels it should be, is one of the most important characteristics of a judge of a court of last resort, from which there is no appeal.

"The Supreme Court, I may say, Mr. President, has been assuming more and more power and infringing more and more on the prerogatives of the legislative branch of the government in recent years.

"Mr. President, this restraint can be acquired only by serving on a court whose decisions are subject to review."

Very recently, in the May 18, 1956 issue of *The U. S. News and World Report,* the Honorable James F. Byrnes of South Carolina published an excellent article under the caption: "The Supreme Court Must Be Curbed." Mr. Byrnes, former member of the Senate and the House, former Secretary of State, former assistant to the President, former member of the Supreme Court of the United States, and holder of almost every public and political honor in his home State of South Carolina, is eminently qualified to speak on this subject. We may be sure that a man of his position would not advocate "curbing" the Supreme Court unless the need for such action were great and immediate.

Our Supreme Court justices should be dedicated solely to the principles of deciding cases according to the Constitution and the law. They should be willing to abstain from legislating and leave that duty to the legislative branches of the government. They should interpret the Constitution without trying to amend it. They should not embark upon social reforms but should leave that to the people.

As one suggestion, *future appointments to the Supreme Court might be limited to persons having had judicial experience* and preferably experience on the federal appellate bench. The High Court *should never be used as a reward for political or financial favor nor as a place of political cold storage* for some potential candidate, possibly a competing candidate for public office. The Constitution clearly indicated that the functions of the Court should be only judicial, not legislative. These functions obviously can be performed best by trained legal and judicial minds. We should be satisfied with nothing less than the best in our highest Court.

Other Suggestions

As suggested earlier, one possible "legal means" of undoing the damage done by the Supreme Court might well be a great campaign to acquaint the people of the United States with the true facts concerning the moral and legal aspects of integration of the races in the schools. This program of education should not stop there but should include a thorough analysis of the facts and the law applicable to the numerous other subjects upon which the present Court has departed from constitutional authority.

There has been a tendency in many quarters to view with alarm the many recent decisions of the Supreme Court and then to shrug off the whole matter by an attitude of, "We can't defy the law and the Supreme Court." This attitude does not comport with the "never-say-die" spirit of this republic. As has been pointed out many times, there is not and never has been a law requiring forced integration of the races in the public schools of the South. The Supreme Court cannot enact such a law, and such a law has not been enacted by any legislative authority.

It is not "defying the Supreme Court" to contest an erroneous and unconstitutional decision of that Court; rather, it is a solemn duty of every citizen, and particularly every lawyer, to take every legal means to correct such erroneous decisions and to protect our Constitution from judicial amendment.

In the early days of our national history, the colonists were presented with the accomplished fact that "His Majesty King George has spoken." Our answer to that was contained in the immortal words of the Declaration of Independence. A portion of that answer has particular significance here. After setting forth the grievances against the crown, the signers of the Declaration of Independence declared: "That these United Colonies are, and of right ought to be, free and independent States." Every constitutional provision and every statute subsequently enacted gave life and meaning to that Declaration. Our loyalty to that principle is only skin-deep if we are content to sit idly by and see our basic laws destroyed by unchecked judicial interpretation.

The battle for constitutional government can be lost if the State and local courts, legislative and administrative officers meekly surrender. The decisions of any court bind only the litigants in that case. If the Supreme Court of the United States orders enforced integration in a suit pending before it in a particular school in Alabama, that does not mean that all other schools in Alabama or in the South must comply with the Court's decree in that case. Yet we read of some instances where local authorities who are not even involved in litigation jump the gun and say, "We reluctantly bow to the decision of the Supreme Court." *If the decision is wrong, it should be contested at every step, from every school, through every court, until the court reaches a correct constitutional conclusion.*

Let us suppose that one of these N.A.A.C.P. cases, which should be summarily dismissed under the Eleventh Amendment, were submitted to a trial court which sincerely believed the Supreme Court decision to be wrong. What a fine start it might be toward reversing the Brown case if such trial court would say: "I cannot reconcile the recent holding of the Supreme Court with the Tenth Amendment of the Constitution of the United States. I am aware that the Supreme Court is the federal court of last resort, and I am aware that the Supreme Court historically has the recognized authority to overrule former decisions of that Court. However, such reversals should be based upon cogent and compelling reasons and authority. I prefer to base my opinion upon the solid authority of Plessy *vs.* Ferguson and the many cases before and after that case which proclaim the same principles.

"I am aware of the doctrine of *stare decisis,* and I do not believe I am departing therefrom. On the other hand, I believe that it is the Supreme Court which has departed therefrom. I cannot, in good conscience, render any decision which I honestly believe is in conflict with the Constitution of the United States and with the generally accepted and declared interpretation of that document for almost a hundred years. Based upon these interpretations, the people in various sections of this country have enacted laws and have developed a culture and a way of life consistent therewith. The destruction of these institutions should not be lightly undertaken. I, therefore, respectfully disagree with the Supreme Court, and I trust that, when this case goes up on appeal, the Supreme Court will reverse its former decision.

"I realize that this opinion may subject me to great criticism. Any criticism or punishment could be borne with fortitude in the knowledge that I had delivered one blow for constitutional government."

Interposition

Another "legal means" of combating the Supreme Court's assumption of legislative power is the "interposition" of the sovereignty of the several States affected. Space will not permit a lengthy discussion of this interesting subject. In brief, it simply means that the State asserts that it has the constitutional right, under the Ninth and Tenth Amendments, to assume full jurisdiction with reference to the question involved and that its jurisdiction is superior to the authority claimed by the federal government. This would appear to be a remedy of last resort. It is difficult, indeed, to believe that the collective conscience of any section of this nation could require some of the States of the Union to go to such lengths to preserve their hard-won and long-established constitutional rights.

Earlier, we referred to the legislation enacted or pending in the southern States concerning the abandonment of the public-school system and the leasing of school facilities to private schools. These statutes are part, but not all, of the policy of interposition already under way. The States of Alabama, Georgia, Mississippi, South Carolina, and Virginia have already adopted resolutions and enacted statutes which announce to the world in no uncertain terms that these States consider the decision of the Supreme Court in the school-segregation cases, and all similar decisions, to be null and void. Some of these States have already passed numerous laws designed to assert their rights under the Tenth Amendment. Undoubtedly, other southern States will take the same or similar steps. These legislative declarations by the several States, which apparently are unknown to, or ignored in, the other States of the Union, are not couched in the soft terms of diplomacy. They state the hard fact that the Supreme Court of the United States has exceeded its authority under the Constitution and has created a condition which these States will not tolerate. Proof of this statement is contained in the Georgia Resolution adopted by the 1956 Session of the General Assembly of that State, portions of which declare:

That the General Assembly of Georgia denies that the Supreme Court of the United States had the right which it asserted in the school cases decided by it on May 17, 1954 to enlarge the language and meaning of the compact by the States in an effort to withdraw from the States powers reserved to them and as daily exercised by them for almost a century;

That the question of contested power has arisen; the Supreme Court of the United States asserts, for its part, that the States did in fact prohibit unto themselves the power to maintain racially separate public institutions, and the State of Georgia, for its part, asserts that it and its sister States have never surrendered such right;

That this assertion upon the part of the Supreme Court of the United States, accompanied by threats of coercion and compulsion against the sovereign States of this Union, constitutes a deliberate, palpable, and dangerous attempt by the Court to prohibit to the States certain rights and powers never surrendered by them;

That the General Assembly of Georgia asserts that whenever the general government attempts to engage in the deliberate, palpable, and dangerous exercise of powers not granted to it, the States who are parties to the compact have the right, and are in duty bound, to interpose for arresting the progress of the evil, and for maintaining, within their respective limits, the authorities, rights and liberties appertaining to them. . . .

THEREFORE, BE IT RESOLVED BY THE HOUSE OF REPRESENTATIVES, THE SENATE CONCURRING:

First: That said decisions and orders of the Supreme Court of the United States relating to separation of the races in the public institutions of a State as announced and promulgated by said Court on May 17, 1954, and May 31, 1955, are null, void, and of no force or effect:

Second: That hereby there is declared the firm intention of this State to take all appropriate measures honorably and constitutionally available to the State to avoid this illegal encroachment upon the rights of her people. . . .

The "Compact" referred to in the first paragraph above is the Constitution of the United States, which was an agreement or compact by and among the separate and "sovereign" States referred to in the Declaration of Independence. This compact, when adopted, became the fundamental law of the land as the Constitution.

These solemn declarations of principle would, of themselves, fill a volume. A reading of them is strongly recommended for all who would avert a catastrophe that now appears imminent.

The time has already arrived when it must be recognized that these declarations are serious expressions, made after due deliberation, by the leaders of a great section of this country. It is also imperative that we recognize, before it is too late, the eternal rightness of their positions.

Interposition is not new in our history, but fortunately, ways have been found to preserve the sovereignty of States without sacrificing the Constitution. The present dilemma is not only the most serious threat that has arisen, calling for the doctrine of interposition, but is also the most serious threat to the Constitution itself. Interposition should be the last resort. All other legal methods should be tried first. If the last resort must be used, and if it fails, then the Constitution has failed.

There may be no turning back when, and if, the States embark upon a defense of interposition. Such a program is now in its beginning. It may be much later than we think. Let us fervently hope that reason and tolerance may arrive in time to extinguish the flames before they engulf all of us.

We need no new approach to old problems. We need to pursue honestly the search for the true facts and to allow truth and experience to be our guideposts.

The last great hope on earth for free institutions of government ultimately rests in the hearts of the people. There must be a reawakening of our forefathers' burning desire for a representative government of checks and balances. This renewed devotion to historic principles must begin in our homes and schools. It must extend to, and embrace, every medium of public information, every public servant, and every private citizen.

Our liberties are too precious to trust to the whim and caprice of courts acting without the restraints of constitutions approved by the people. The challenge to this generation is to insure that *government of law* and not of men *shall prevail.*